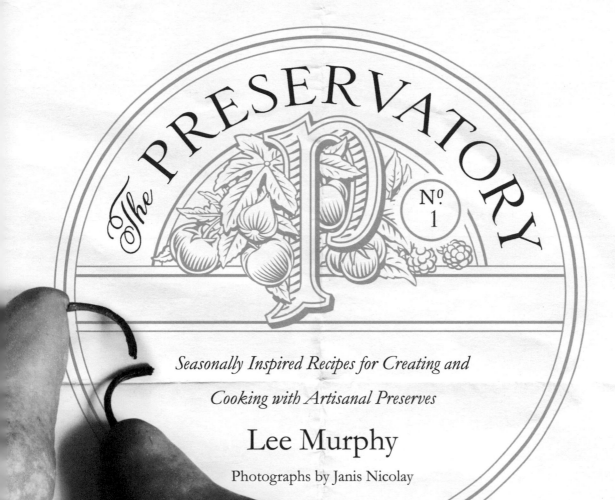

The PRESERVATORY

№ 1

Seasonally Inspired Recipes for Creating and

Cooking with Artisanal Preserves

Lee Murphy

Photographs by Janis Nicolay

appetite
by RANDOM HOUSE

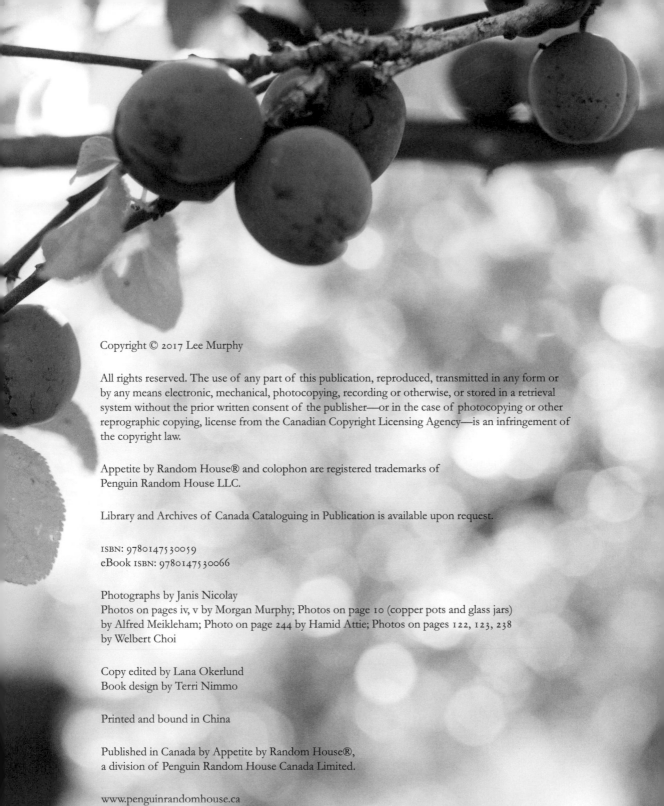

Appetite by Random House® and colophon are registered trademarks of Penguin Random House LLC.

Library and Archives of Canada Cataloguing in Publication is available upon request.

ISBN: 9780147530059
eBook ISBN: 9780147530066

Photographs by Janis Nicolay
Photos on pages iv, v by Morgan Murphy; Photos on page 10 (copper pots and glass jars) by Alfred Meikleham; Photo on page 244 by Hamid Attie; Photos on pages 122, 123, 238 by Welbert Choi

Copy edited by Lana Okerlund
Book design by Terri Nimmo

Printed and bound in China

Published in Canada by Appetite by Random House®, a division of Penguin Random House Canada Limited.

www.penguinrandomhouse.ca

10 9 8 7 6 5 4 3 2 1

appetite
by RANDOM HOUSE | Penguin
Random
House

For Gracie

CONTENTS

FOREWORD

BY LESLEY STOWE

From the moment I met Lee her enthusiasm for great food and the sharing of it was immediate, so it was no surprise when she revealed that she was working on a cookbook. This is not just a collection of recipes but a sharing of the experiences that are the very heart of The Preservatory and Lee's philosophy. The journey she takes you on in showing how and why she got into the world of preserves will change the way you think about preserves and make you appreciate what a truly artisan business she has created.

Lee lives and breathes everything she has captured in this cookbook. Not only does she make, market and sell preserves both sweet and savory, she actually grows a lot of the fruit that goes into these preserves on her own property. Now *that* is dedication, drive and craziness. Who grows 50 varieties of tomatoes in a 500-square-foot greenhouse!

Lee and I share many things in common, but one that stands out is an absolute passion and commitment to creating great products and standing behind them, using the finest quality ingredients available and only using those ingredients when they are at their best.

This book sings that philosophy through every chapter and encourages you to cook with the seasons to achieve great results.

Even if you never thought of yourself as a jam maker, the "I barely have time to make dinner" type, do yourself a favor and start with one recipe. Go to your local farmer's market and choose your favorite fruit that is in season. As Lee says, picking the best, perfectly ripe fruit is the single most important step in the preserving process. She will step by step guide you through producing something amazing, whether it is a Rhubarb & Vanilla preserve (now a staple in my fridge all year), or the Spicy Sweet Charred Onion & Figs—perfect for an instant hors d'oeuvre.

In her pairing suggestions, a hugely helpful fruit guide, and a chapter on tools and equipment, Lee draws you into her world, bringing preserve making and all its uses to centre stage. Preserves are no longer that jar that just comes out in the morning for toast and scones but comes into play in everything from appetizers and marinades to desserts.

Lee is always creating, pushing the boundaries of what can be possible, and lucky for us has chosen to share her wealth of knowledge and hours of research and development on preserves in this gorgeous, inspirational book.

This collection of recipes and the tales of their creation should give you many happy hours of reading and even more hours in the kitchen creating; Lee knows of what she writes: Good Fruit = Good Jam.

INTRODUCTION

I f someone had told me in July 1997, when we purchased the property on 4th Avenue in Langley, British Columbia, that seventeen years later I would travel to London to check stock and plan demos for our preserves in Harrods—I would have said "where's Harrods?" and then "what preserves?" Seriously—jam . . . who knew? Opening my own business creating and selling preserves wasn't some lifelong dream I had. In fact, this all began with a horse. A beautiful two-year-old Bay Arabian named Rico. I was smitten from the time he launched himself out of the horse trailer and into my life, and from then on I drove forty-five minutes out to Langley almost every day to see him. Deciding I wanted to be closer to him (oh, and save money on boarding, which is a total misconception), my husband, Patrick, and I began to look for a little piece of land for all of us. We found the ideal location—five acres on Campbell Valley Park—with horse trails galore and a view of Golden Ears Mountain Range. We proceeded to build our dream home (we are still proceeding, but I'm sure it will be finished one day) and a horse barn (actually we built the barn first—priorities, you know!). We lived in a fifth-wheel trailer with our one-year-old son and three-year-old daughter while we built—this taught me patience and how to cook in a very confined space for five months, both of which I think have served me well while creating this crazy lifestyle business.

After a few years of baby raising, I was trying to find a creative outlet that would pay some bills and allow me to stay at home with these amazing kids. I started a small gift basket company with my mum, Mary. I loved all the creative specialty foods we were bringing in and kept thinking, I should be making these myself! When we sold the business five years later, after one particularly long Christmas season, I decided I really wanted to try to do something new. I convinced Patrick I needed a greenhouse and that we'd be able to sell enough from it to get our farm status and reduce our property taxes. The glass greenhouse was built and I began trying my hand at growing culinary herbs and became obsessed with heirloom tomatoes—one year, I grew more than fifty varieties!

That same year, we took a trip to Paris—my first ever to Europe—and I tasted Christine Ferber's jams for the first time: my aha moment in Oprah speak. Paris's vibrant markets, the *fromageries* (where they asked what *time* I'd be eating the cheese before choosing one), the bakeries (going down into the hot basement of Poilâne to see them pulling baguettes out of the wood-fired ovens and into the back room to watch the ancient apple peeler prep the fruit for their beyond flaky apple tarts) were all inspirational and pivotal for this new business (ad)venture I was embarking on. I remember coming home, and on a trip to our local grocery store actually feeling a bit weepy when I saw the "baguettes," knowing full well that Paris had ruined me.

Later that year we built our carriage house and it housed our cooking school with a B&B attached. We started selling our wares at farmers' markets and direct marketing the cooking classes and B&B. The B&B didn't last very long, maybe a year—that's a story for another book! On the bright side, our orchard was beginning to take shape and I quickly realized that adding value to the fruit would be a more sustainable model than selling apples by the pound. Before I knew it our artisanal preserves were outselling everything else we were loading onto the truck.

Over the next two years I continued to create preserves for each season, and one copper pot quickly grew to six. I began to obsess about flavor combining and before I knew it, we had more than twenty-four offerings. From the beginning we made our preserves seasonally, and the hardest part was convincing customers that they couldn't have strawberry in December. We try not to run out each year; sometimes we make enough, and other times peach is sold out by October. Using the fruit at its peak is the one true secret to jam making—I've never used "jam" fruit (the flat of berries too soft to sell at the end of the market day). The natural pectin left in overripe fruit is little to none and makes an inferior product. My philosophy is, if I won't eat it, I won't use it for jam, is just one way we make sure we are producing the best jam with each and every kettle.

It was also in 2004 that my good friend Glenys Morgan came to me with an opportunity that I originally turned down. Glenys was one of my favorite guest chefs who came and taught at our cooking studio. She told me about a scholarship for a new cooking school opening in Vancouver and thought I should take some time to pursue my passion more seriously. I was already run off my feet with kids, farm, business and life in general, but that night over a glass (or two) of wine decided, "if not now, when?" and called Glenys the next day and said YES! I continued the cooking classes at the farm, the farmers' markets and making the preserves while attending Northwest Culinary Academy—it was hard work, and I *loved* it. With culinary diploma in hand I started catering from the carriage house kitchen and developed more offerings for our Farmgate Market, which the carriage house eventually morphed into. The market for the preserves grew rapidly and we decided to automate a few of the steps—namely filling, capping and labeling, which led to building the Preservatory in 2012. We transformed the main floor of the carriage house and built our "micro" production facility below the existing commercial kitchen, which I now use for recipe testing and basically playing with my food. Creating the Preservatory increased our capacity while saving all of us a life of carpal tunnel syndrome from all the ladling and cap twisting.

Oh, the reality of living the dream . . . not for the faint of heart or the lazy of body! No rest for the wicked, they say—gotta work on the wicked part a bit I think. A cookbook seemed like the next logical step. *The Preservatory* is a collection of recipes for and with preserves—aka Fancy Jams. Many of these recipes are inspired by travels, meals shared and friends gained on this crazy ride. I hope you get the pages sticky . . . just PLEASE wipe the jars! —*Lee*

THE FRUIT

The fruit we use at Vista D'oro is truly the star of all of our preserves; choosing the best, perfectly ripe fruit is the single most important step in the preserving process. Good fruit in, good jam out!

At the Preservatory we use only fruit in its prime—fresh-picked, perfectly sun-ripened fruit. Fruit has the most pectin just as it ripens, so you're better off using fruit that is the slightest bit under-ripe rather than overripe, as the pectin begins to deteriorate from that perfect point of ripeness on. The fruit on sale at the end of the day at a farmers' market is not the fruit you want for jam making. If you don't have the time or energy to make jam at the time of perfect ripeness, simply freeze the fruit for when you do.

Local fruit is best, as you can trust that it's been picked ripe and not green for shipping; sun-ripened fruit is so much more flavorful. Get to know your farmers, create good relationships and you'll be the first they call when they have something extra special or just an abundance that would otherwise go to waste.

I'd much rather spend a few more pennies per pound on grade A fruit than have to pick through blemished, moldy fruit.

By this point I'm sure you can tell I'm a wee bit obsessive about the fruit we process on the farm. We grow most of it, and I'm pretty particular about that which we don't grow. I honestly think that what makes our preserves different is not the flavors, not the story, but the fruit we use. It shines through in each jar we make, and I don't take that or the farmers who grow our fruit for granted.

For preserve-making purposes we think of our fruit in two different groups: the high-pectin happy-to-jam fruit and the low-pectin not-really-feelin'-it fruit. On page 21 we've shared our secret for working with the more challenging of the two.

HAPPY-TO-JAM FRUIT

Apples	*Plums*
Apricots	*Raspberries*
Blackberries	*Rhubarb*
Citrus	*Tomatillos*
Crabapples	*Tomatoes (green unripe)*
Cranberries	

NOT-REALLY-FEELIN'-IT FRUIT

Blueberries	*Pears*
Cherries	*Pineapples*
Figs	*Rhubarb*
Mango	*Strawberries*
Melons	*Tomatoes* (other than green unripe; and
Peaches	yes, they're a fruit!)

Farmer Patrick (my husband) likes to say that we're "growing Langley fruit and selling it around the world!" We are so fortunate to have a steady flow of available fruit right here on the farm, beginning in early June and lasting until late October.

Here's a snapshot of what's growin' on at Vista D'oro . . .

APPLES

Belle de Boskoop—Large, firm, juicy, tart, yellow-red blush;
Preservatory crew favorite!

Braeburn—Bi-colored, great flavor

Cox's Orange Pippin—Large orange-red apples of exceptional quality;
old English

Fuji—Excellent eating apple with yellow-green skin

Gravenstein—Great flavor, red stripes on green fruit, firm and juicy;
old German

Haralred—Hardy with tart, dark red apples

Idared—Good keeper, mild apple flavor

Jonagold—Large fruit, red stripes on yellow skin, firm, crispy and juicy

Liberty—Dwarf, good eating and my personal favorite

Mutsu—Large, yellow, crispy, juicy fruit; good coastal apple; heavy bearer

Northern Spy—Greenish-yellow apple with a red blush and rich aromatic flavor

Royal Gala—Medium-sized, firm, bright red fruit

Heritage—Five lovely 100-year-old heritage trees

ASIAN PEARS

Chojuro—Good flavor, round fruit; one of the best

Hosui—Large, golden-russet fruit with crispy, sugary flesh; good keeper;
best-flavored Asian pear

20th Century—aka Nijisseiki; greenish-yellow; sweet, juicy flesh

21st Century—aka Kikusui; round; not pretty but very juicy

BLACKBERRIES

The meanest, most delicious crop of wild blackberries around!

CHERRIES

Bing—Large, sweet, deep red fruit; firm and juicy

Black Tartarian—Large, dark fruit; sweet, full flavor

Queen Anne—Similar to Rainier, but a little tarter

Rainier—Golden-yellow with red-blush shoulders; sweet and delicate flavor

Stella—Large, flavorful fruit; good for canning

Sweetheart—Bright red, medium-sized, flavorful fruit

Van—Hardy, sweet black cherry; bears heavily and resists cracking

CRABAPPLES

Heritage Dolgo—One of the best crabapples for jelly making

ENGLISH WALNUTS

Three towering 100-year-old trees and one struggling runt!

GRAPES	*Dornfelder*—Red varietal developed in Germany
	Léon Millot—Red hybrid varietal created in Alsace in 1911
	Marechal Foch—Named after a French marshal; a red hybrid that ripens well in our wet climate; intense in flavor and color
	Ortega—Very aromatic, delicious white varietal; a cross between Siegerrebe and Müller-Thurgau
	Pinot Gris—White grape thought to be a mutant clone of Pinot Noir; yes, the grape of Pinot Grigio!
	Schönburger—A lovely German white varietal; early ripening for our cool climate
	Siegerrebe—A German white varietal with a taste similar to Gewürztraminer

PEARS	*Anjou*—Sweet juicy fruit; winter pear
	Bartlett—Quintessential pear flavor
	Bosc—Green, long-neck winter pear; juicy white flesh; very sweet
	Clapp's Favorite—Large, bright yellow fruit; very sweet and productive trees
	Red Bartlett—Early ripening; floral pear flavor
	Heritage—One lovely 100-year-old heritage tree

PLUMS	*Blue Damson*—Small, round, dark purple skin, freestone; good for jams/jellies
	Burbank—Hardy and early ripening fruit
	Early Italian—Same as Italian, but ripens two weeks earlier
	Greengage—Medium-sized, round, greenish skin, good pollenizer
	Italian—European prune plum, purple skin, yellow flesh, freestone
	Peach—Medium-large fruit, semi-freestone, sweet flavor, productive
	Santa Rosa—Deep red-purple fruit, golden flesh, rich flavor
	Satsuma—Maroon over green skin, sweet flesh
	Shiro Yellow—Sweet, juicy, good producer

| SOUR CHERRIES | *Evans*—aka Bali; does very well in our cooler, wet climate |
| | *Montmorency*—Light in color; one of the most popular varieties |

| TOMATOES | *About 30 varieties of heirloom tomatoes* |

That list explains why it's a madhouse around here during harvest! The rest of the fruit we use is from our great farmer friends who grow berries in the Fraser Valley and stone fruits in the Similkameen Valley. We are so fortunate to live in British Columbia, where the abundance of fruit is staggering. It makes my job as jam maker so much easier!

"The ideal fruit jelly will quiver, not flow, when removed from its mold . . ."

NELLIE ESTHER GOLDTHWAITE

The Principles of Jelly Making

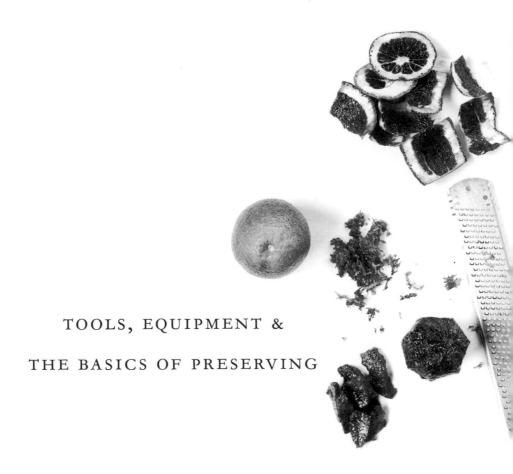

TOOLS, EQUIPMENT &

THE BASICS OF PRESERVING

TOOLS & EQUIPMENT

This is a bit of a wish list, and you don't need to have it all if you're just starting out in this crazy, wonderful world of preserving. It's far better to start with what you have on hand and work your way toward a good arsenal of jam-making equipment than it is to break the bank on tools you end up using only a handful of times.

ESSENTIALS

Copper jam pot—Once you've used a proper copper jam pot, you'll never go back. It's a bit of an investment, but worth every copper penny—see what I did there? Alternatively, you can use a stainless-steel saucepan, as wide as it is deep, with a heavy, thick bottom plate to ensure even cooking. Be sure the pan is large enough to allow the fruit to boil up and not over. Sloping sides are ideal, allowing for quicker reduction of the jam, less cooking time and a fruitier-tasting product.

Scale—A must-have piece of equipment and not a big investment. Small digital scales are so inexpensive now, and without one you won't be able to make preserves consistently or safely. Added bonus: your baking will benefit as well!

Candy thermometer—Digital is best, and be sure that the temperature scale reaches beyond 230°F.

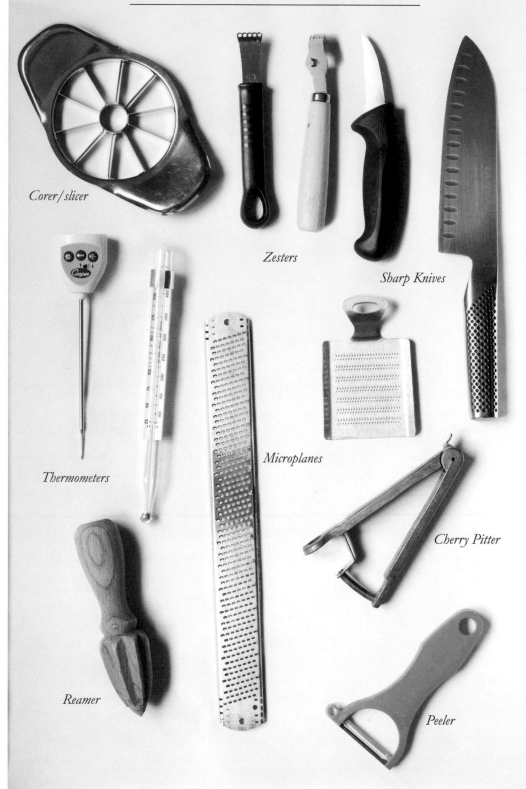

Corer/slicer

Zesters

Sharp Knives

Thermometers

Microplanes

Cherry Pitter

Reamer

Peeler

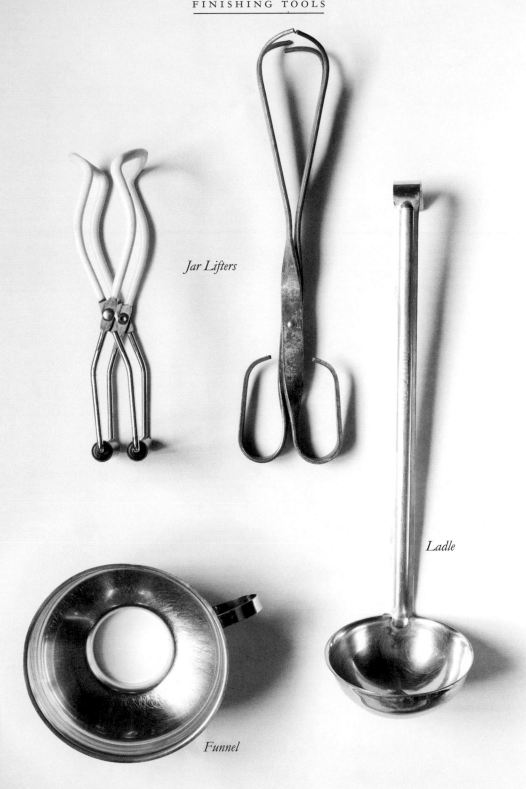

Jar Lifters

Ladle

Funnel

Heatproof spatulas.

Canning jars and lids.

Small-hole slotted spoon—For skimming preserves.

Ladle—For filling the jars.

Funnel—For dripless filling of the jars.

Jar lifter—For pulling the jars out of the canning pot.

Large stock or canning pot—For processing jars after filling.

Baking sheets—For sterilizing jars in the oven and roasting fruit.

Sharp knives—Chef's and paring knives. The only thing you'll be able to cut with a dull
        knife is your finger.

Corer/slicer—To core apples and pears, or use a sharp knife.

Peeler—For peeling fruit.

Zester—For zesting citrus fruits.

Microplane—For finely grated zest.

Mortar and pestle—For spices and peppercorns.

Cheesecloth and kitchen string—To make spice removal easier.

Tea infuser—For easy retrieval of spices and peppercorns.

Colander—For rinsing fruit.

Stainless-steel sieve—To strain fruits out of their syrup.

Parchment paper—For roasting fruits and covering macerating fruit.

Cherry pitter—For cherries, believe it or not ;).

Juicer or reamer—For all the lemon juice you'll need.

Cutting boards—Pretty self-explanatory, no?

Bowls—Stainless and ceramic for macerating fruit.

Glass measuring cups—Small and large.

Set of measuring spoons.

Tea Infuser

THE BASICS OF PRESERVING

The ideal fruit jelly will quiver, not flow,
when removed from its mold; a product with texture so tender
that it cuts easily with a spoon, and yet so firm that
the angles thus produced retain their shape; a clear product that
is neither syrupy, gummy, sticky nor tough; neither is it
brittle and yet it will break, and does this with distinct beautiful
cleavage which leaves sparkling characteristic faces.
—NELLIE ESTHER GOLDTHWAITE,
The Principles of Jelly Making, 1911

Jam . . . it's a bit of a Zen thing. There is no way to rush the process, and it's a great way to slow down the rhythm of the day. Standing over a bubbly pot of fruit is mesmerizing. Watching the transformation from fresh, ripe fruit to jewel-toned, glossy jam is addictive. You can see how the jam changes at each stage in the process: from big bubbles, to smaller bubbles, then bubbles in the bubbles and the fruit falling into the syrup . . . before you know it, you won't need the thermometer or cold plate to tell you when the jam is ready for the jar—the jam will tell you. Sounds a little hippy-dippy, as my dad would say, but jam making really can be a relaxing, not to mention rewarding, endeavor.

A QUICK WORD OF ADVICE ON MEASURING YOUR FRUIT

When the recipe calls for five pounds of fruit, consider it as five pounds of prepped and ready-to-make-into-jam fruit. Keep that in mind when buying your fruit and be sure to calculate waste into your requirements depending on the fruit. For instance, for berry recipes you'll need only about 3 to 5 percent more to allow for a couple of mushy berries; however, for citrus fruits you'll need closer to 30 to 40 percent extra to allow for removal of peels and pith. I've given an approximate gross weight in each recipe as a guide.

STANDARD STEPS FOR PRESERVING

While not all preserves are created equal, most are the result of a standard set of steps.

1. Source the best, perfectly ripe fruit. Good fruit = good jam.
2. *Mise en place.* Have everything in its place before you start—the secret to all great kitchens.
3. Prepare the fruit to the desired size and shape.
4. Add sugar and lemon juice.
5. Add flavorings, such as herbs, spices or wine.
6. **Pre-Jam/Two-Cook/or Straight to It!** (more on this below).
7. Cook quickly at high heat to set at 220°F (more on this below).
8. Test for set (aka the consistency of the jam).
9. Place hot jam into hot sterilized jars, leaving only a ¼ inch of headspace in the jar.
10. Wipe any drips off the rims of the jars and screw on sterilized lids tightly.
11. Process in a water bath.

At the Preservatory we use three methods of jam-making, as mentioned in step 6 above, and each has its own place in our repertoire, depending on the fruit we're working with.

Some fruits, especially rhubarb and strawberries, require a soft touch and do best with an overnight maceration in sugar and lemon juice to draw out all their lovely juices and soften the fruit before cooking—we call this **Pre-Jammin'.** At this point you have the option of throwing the mixture in the freezer. If going straight to jar, we strain off the accumulated juices and bring those to a boil before adding the fruit back in and bringing the preserves to set. This helps the fruit retain some shape and also keeps it from caramelizing.

For many low-pectin fruits such as Blueberry, Pear and Tomato, we use the **Two-Cook** method in which we bring the ingredients up to a boil, cool and refrigerate overnight. Again, this is where you can pop the mixture in the freezer for future use or complete the process by bringing the preserve to set. This method helps retain the fresh flavor and texture and ensures a better set for these "not-really-feelin' it" fruit by gently taking them from fresh to jar.

At the Preservatory we fill the freezers with these *pre-jam or two-cook* containers of prepared fruit at times when much of the fruit on the farm seems to be ready all in the same week!

Of course we all love the **Straight to It** process, which, as it sounds, is simply a matter of throwing everything in the jam pot and cooking to set—"Happy-to-jam" fruit like raspberries and cranberries are a Preservatory favorite for this reason.

Testing for set, otherwise known as the consistency of the jam, is key to ensuring a great product. A simple way of testing is to keep a stack of small plates in your freezer when you're making jam. Once the preserve comes to temperature at 220°F, simply drop a small amount of the hot preserve onto the cold plate, wait a couple of

Add sugar.

Add flavorings.

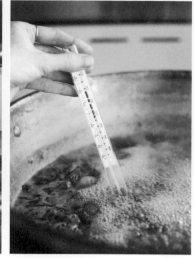

Set at 220° F.

Test for set.

Hot jars out of the oven.

Fill hot jars.

Process in a water bath.

Enjoy!

"Using fruit at
its peak is the
one true secret to
jam-making."

minutes and then tilt the plate. If the preserve moves very slowly, or not at all, it's ready to go into the jar. If the preserve runs freely across the plate, continue cooking. Just make sure to keep checking every three to five minutes so you don't overcook the batch.

Another good rule of thumb is to preserve seasonally if you can. Following the seasons really does connect us to Mother Nature. Here on the farm it's a little easier to stick to this rule, as we do it out of necessity, but in the kitchen, even though you can choose to do strawberry jam in the winter, your preserves will be so much more delicious if you stick to jammin' in season.

Jam making is truly not rocket science, and it can become an obsessive hobby if you're not careful.

SAFETY

A word or two about safety: Preserves are considered a low-risk product for processing due to their high sugar content, pH levels and the high heat at which the preserves are jarred. But even though they are low risk, a few precautions are essential in keeping them that way.

1. First, sterilize EVERYTHING! Boil the lids, tongs, ladles . . . everything that will touch your product. You can boil your jars for 15 to 20 minutes, or simply place the clean jars in the oven at 225°F for thirty minutes to sterilize.
2. Next, the sugar. Always use the correct amount of sugar. Sugar is for preservation and gelling, and reducing the amount you use changes the nature of the preserves and opens the door for bacteria and mold to grow—ick!
3. Lastly, acid. Lemon juice provides the acid required to balance the pH of the preserves, and it activates the gelling process.

Together, these three factors—sterilization, sugar and acid—will ensure you're making a safe and delicious product that will last months, if not years, on the shelf.

In addition, always check your lids to ensure a properly sealed jar. Concave = good. Convex = bad. If your jar does not seal, simply store it in the fridge and use the preserves within three months.

HOW TO PROCESS PRESERVES

Processing jars is a way to ensure a longer shelf life of your hard work, and the extra step is easy.

1. Simply fill a stockpot or canner halfway with water and bring to a boil.
2. Using a jar lifter, carefully lower filled jars into the hot water (they should have at least one inch of water above them) and bring back to a boil.
3. Boil for 10 to 20 minutes, depending on recipe, starting the timer once boiling begins.
4. Remove carefully using jar lifter.

STORAGE OF PRESERVES

The best place to store all your hard work is in a dry, dark, cool spot—the back of the pantry works well. Typically, preserves are best if used within the year; after that, the fruity flavors and colors start to break down slightly.

LOW-PECTIN FRUITS

Low-pectin fruits are often the bane of many would-be jam makers, due to their reluctance to setting up nicely, but they don't have to be! A simple, proven method we use at the Preservatory is the addition of a fresh-cooked apple juice using green (unripe) apples (see recipe on opposite page). Do up a nice big batch and keep it in your freezer in smaller containers so you'll have some on hand whenever you're making preserves with low-pectin fruits that need a little help to set.

TIPS & TRICKS

*All those lemons you're juicing: zest them first, sprinkle the zest
with a little sugar and freeze the zest for use in muffins,
scones and stir-fries. Save any and all extra chopped fruit in the freezer for easy
smoothie prep. Juice lemons over a sieve to catch the seeds.
When adding alcohol to your hot preserves, be sure to add it off the flame
and pour in carefully as it will cause the mixture to bubble up and splatter.
Use vinegars sparingly when cooking in copper, as it will react.
If you want to use more vinegar, use a stainless steel jam pot instead.*

{YIELDS APPROXIMATELY 5 ½ LITERS}

"Fresh" Apple Juice

To help set preserves made with low-pectin fruit, this is a simple addition—and our secret weapon. Make sure to use green, unripe apples if you can find them; otherwise, a tart Granny Smith will do as well. Note: In a pinch you could use a completely unfiltered apple juice from your farmers' market.

7 lb green apples (stems removed), quartered

12 cups water

1. In a large stockpot, bring apples and water to a boil over high heat; cook until apples are falling apart, about 20 to 30 minutes.

2. In a food processor or food mill, pulse in small batches to create a mash; strain through a sieve or chinois. For a clearer juice, line the sieve with cheesecloth.

3. Freeze in smaller containers for use in preserving recipes. Keeps for six to nine months.

DEFINITIONS

So what's the deal? Is it a jam? A preserve? According to whom? Preserves are commonly categorized in the following way:

Preserves—Containing whole pieces or chunks of fruit.
Conserves—Containing nuts and dried fruit.
Jam—Mashed cooked fruit, spreadable.
Jelly—Clear, juice only, no fruit.
Marmalade—A jelly that contains citrus rind or peel.

At the Preservatory, we call everything we do a *preserve*—jams, jellies, marmalades, even pickles. Basically, we're preserving all of our products for future use. I use *preserve* and *jam* interchangeably throughout this book.

Whatever you decide to call your creations, I hope they are delicious and that you enjoy the journey!

THE JAM MAKER'S ARSENAL OF ADD-INS

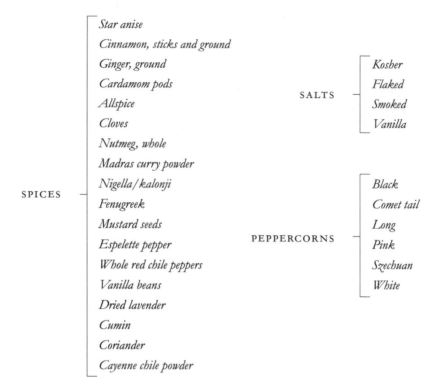

SPICES
- Star anise
- Cinnamon, sticks and ground
- Ginger, ground
- Cardamom pods
- Allspice
- Cloves
- Nutmeg, whole
- Madras curry powder
- Nigella/kalonji
- Fenugreek
- Mustard seeds
- Espelette pepper
- Whole red chile peppers
- Vanilla beans
- Dried lavender
- Cumin
- Coriander
- Cayenne chile powder

SALTS
- Kosher
- Flaked
- Smoked
- Vanilla

PEPPERCORNS
- Black
- Comet tail
- Long
- Pink
- Szechuan
- White

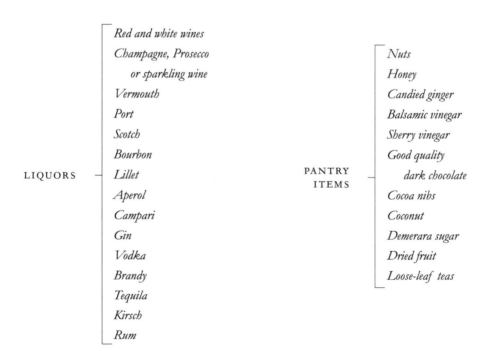

LIQUORS
- Red and white wines
- Champagne, Prosecco or sparkling wine
- Vermouth
- Port
- Scotch
- Bourbon
- Lillet
- Aperol
- Campari
- Gin
- Vodka
- Brandy
- Tequila
- Kirsch
- Rum

PANTRY ITEMS
- Nuts
- Honey
- Candied ginger
- Balsamic vinegar
- Sherry vinegar
- Good quality dark chocolate
- Cocoa nibs
- Coconut
- Demerara sugar
- Dried fruit
- Loose-leaf teas

HOW TO USE THIS BOOK

Part I

Includes recipes FOR preserves, separated into the four seasons, like life on the farm. Each preserve recipe has pairing suggestions as well as three recipe suggestions from Part II. Preserves that we currently make and sell at the Preservatory are shown with "A Preservatory Classic" beneath the title; you can find these on store shelves or online if you feel like skipping the stove—we got you!

Part II

Includes recipes WITH preserves, separated into Brunch, Aperitivo, Dinner, and Dessert. Three perfect preserves are suggested for each of these recipes, and I hope you'll mix and match. These recipes will work just as well with whatever similar fruit jam or preserve you have on hand. Improvise at will! Cheese, Charcuterie, Pickles & Cocktails follow and at the end of Part II you'll find our list of 101 Uses for Jam!

PART I

RECIPES FOR . . .

SPRING

HAPPENING ON THE FARM

Planning, patience and playing in the greenhouse

IN SEASON

Rhubarb, strawberries, cherries, raspberries, blueberries, soft herbs and asparagus

Spring is my favorite season. We have so much to celebrate in the spring: Patrick and I were married in April, and both of our kids were born in May. The greenhouse is gorgeous in the spring, usually full to bursting by the end of April, and the farm is incredibly lush from all the previous months of rain. Spring always feels like a fresh start.

On the farm our spring truly starts no earlier than May, with rhubarb the first to make it to the pot. We do a lot of planning in the early spring while we're waiting patiently for the arrival of that first crop of rhubarb; the gardens, farm events and production for the coming crazy seasons are all organized and scheduled, because once it starts, the madness doesn't stop until late October!

I love the smell of spring—all the herbs coming out of the greenhouse, the warmed soil ready for planting. And let's face it, from November until May we're pretty reliant on not-so-local fruit to keep the pots hot. I do love me some exotic tropical fruits but nothing beats fruit grown on your own farm or one not too far down the road.

Oh, and spring is also the season when we make Strawberry with Pistachio & Vanilla preserve—my new favorite!

SPRING PRESERVES

{YIELDS TEN TO TWELVE 8-OZ/250-ML JARS}

This is the preserve that started it all! I loved selling plants and produce at the market, but the pride I felt selling something I'd made in my kitchen with my own hands became a bit of an addiction. This preserve is the first one I took to farmers' markets back in 2001, and it's still the first one I reach for in my fridge, which, you can probably guess, is literally overflowing with jam options! It has just the right amount of pucker from the tart rhubarb, and the vanilla softens the edges nicely. A heaping tablespoon stirred into cottage cheese is my go-to "diet" breakfast, and when I give up on that craziness, I pile it onto buttermilk scones with Devonshire cream . . . so divine!

RHUBARB & VANILLA
— a Preservatory classic —

5 lb trimmed, chopped rhubarb*   ½ cup fresh lemon juice
1 vanilla bean   4 lb (8 cups) sugar

1. Cut vanilla bean in half lengthwise and scrape out seeds with the dull side of a paring knife. Stir vanilla seeds into lemon juice and whisk to separate seeds.
2. Stir rhubarb together with sugar and vanilla-lemon juice. Macerate mixture overnight in the fridge.
3. The next day, strain accumulated juices into a jam pot. Reserve rhubarb. Boil juice to 220°F. Add rhubarb and bring back to a boil, stirring often to prevent scorching and skimming as required. Cook to set, again to 220°F; check set on a cold plate (see page 16).
4. Let sit 5 minutes, then ladle into hot sterilized jars, wipe rims, place sterilized lids on jars and process 10 to 15 minutes.

* You will need about 6 lb of whole rhubarb.

❧

GREAT WITH THE FOLLOWING RECIPES:
Pan-Seared Duck Breast, 180 | Mum's Buttermilk Scones, 126 | Eton Mess, 205
PERFECT CHEESE PAIRING:
Délice de Bourgogne
OTHER SERVING SUGGESTIONS:
On hot buttered toast | In cottage cheese

The aroma of this combination cooking in the kitchen is seriously heavenly. This versatile preserve is great for both sweet and savory applications. With its hint of Asian flavors, it is as perfect with a store-bought roast duck as it is spooned into a tart shell for a last-minute dessert.

RHUBARB WITH
GINGER & ORANGE ZEST

5 lb trimmed, chopped rhubarb*	1-inch knob fresh ginger, peeled and
4 lb (8 cups) sugar	grated
½ cup fresh lemon juice	Zest and juice of 2 medium oranges

1. Combine rhubarb with sugar, lemon juice, ginger, and orange zest and juice. Macerate overnight in the fridge.
2. The next day, strain accumulated juices into a jam pot. Reserve rhubarb. Boil juice to 220°F. Add rhubarb and bring back to a boil, stirring often to prevent scorching and skimming as required. Cook to set, again to 220°F; check set on a cold plate (see page 16).
3. Let sit 5 minutes, then ladle into hot sterilized jars, wipe rims, place sterilized lids on jars and process 10 to 15 minutes.

* You will need about 6 lb of whole rhubarb.

❦

GREAT WITH THE FOLLOWING RECIPES:

Crispy Pork Belly Bites, 147 | *Roast Lamb & Moroccan Couscous, 177* | *Jam Tartlettes, 211*

PERFECT CHEESE PAIRING:

Manchego

OTHER SERVING SUGGESTIONS:

On roast duck | *In hot tea*

{YIELDS TEN TO TWELVE 8-OZ/250-ML JARS}

I am so happy to have written this cookbook, and this recipe might be the main reason. This combination has been percolating for a while—since, I think, a trip to a *patisserie* in Paris—and from the first test batch it's been love at first taste. There was actually a "YUM" written on the test recipe (not sure who wrote it, but I fully concur).

STRAWBERRY WITH PISTACHIO & VANILLA

5 lb hulled, quartered strawberries*

1 vanilla bean

½ cup fresh lemon juice

4 lb (8 cups) sugar

½ cup shelled pistachios, toasted at 350°F for 5 to 7 minutes, and chopped

1. Cut vanilla bean in half lengthwise and scrape out the seeds with the dull side of a paring knife. Stir vanilla seeds into lemon juice and whisk to separate seeds.
2. Stir berries together with sugar and vanilla-lemon juice. Macerate overnight in the fridge.
3. The next day, strain accumulated juices into a jam pot. Reserve berries. Boil juice to set at 220°F. Add berries and bring back to a boil, skimming often. Cook to set, again to 220°F; check set on a cold plate (see page 16).
4. Add pistachios and bring back to one last boil.
5. Let sit 5 minutes, then ladle into hot sterilized jars, wipe rims, place sterilized lids on jars and process 15 to 20 minutes.

* You will need about 5¼ lb of whole fruit.

GREAT WITH THE FOLLOWING RECIPES:

Eton Mess, 205 | *Bruléed Steel-Cut Oatmeal, 119* | *Brie & Preserve–Stuffed French Toast, 120*

PERFECT CHEESE PAIRING:

Saint-André

OTHER SERVING SUGGESTIONS:

Off a big spoon! | *On ice cream*

{YIELDS TWELVE TO FOURTEEN 8-OZ/250-ML JARS}

You know spring is here to stay once this one is in the pot. Afternoon tea in the garden is the perfect locale to enjoy this preserve. Stand over this preserve while it's bubbling away and you won't need perfume for a week! Inspiration hit after a long wait in line at Berthillon, the BEST little ice cream shop in Paris. The strawberry rose was almost as delicious as the salted caramel . . . well worth the wait in line. Rose petals are available at some organic growers, but if you can't find them, rosewater will sufficiently flavor this preserve.

STRAWBERRY & ROSES

5 lb hulled, quartered strawberries*

4 lb (8 cups) sugar

½ cup fresh lemon juice

½ cup rose water

2 cups fresh rose petals, unsprayed
(optional)

1. Wash, hull and chop berries. Stir berries together with sugar, lemon juice and rose water. Macerate overnight in the fridge.
2. The next day, strain accumulated juices into a jam pot. Reserve berries. Boil juice to set at 220°F. Add berries and bring back to a boil. Be careful, as this one foams up fast; you may have to lower the heat for a bit and skim often. Cook to set, again to 220°F; check set on a cold plate (see page 16).
3. Gently stir in rose petals, then bring back to one last boil.
4. Let sit 5 to 10 minutes, then ladle into hot sterilized jars, wipe rims, place sterilized lids on jars and process 10 to 20 minutes.

* You will need about 5¼ lb of whole fruit.

❧

GREAT WITH THE FOLLOWING RECIPES:

Glazed Almond & Polenta Cake, 192 | *Queen of Puddings, 209* | *Best Crepes Ever! 128*

PERFECT CHEESE PAIRING:

Chèvre

OTHER SERVING SUGGESTIONS:

In yogurt | *On rice pudding*

{YIELDS TEN TO TWELVE 8-OZ/250-ML JARS}

I know, I know . . . another strawberry recipe. Trust me, this one stands alone. Roasting the strawberries takes them to a completely different level, and the addition of mint doesn't hurt either. It's also a great way to make a spring preserve in the winter with less-than-perfect fruit, if you just can't wait. Added bonus: it makes THE best mojito.

ROASTED STRAWBERRY & MINT

5 lb hulled and halved strawberries*
4 lb (8 cups) sugar, divided
½ cup fresh lemon juice
1 cup chopped fresh mint leaves

1. Preheat oven to 375°F.
2. Lay out strawberries cut side up on a parchment-lined baking sheet, sprinkle with 2 Tbsp sugar and roast approximately 15 minutes, just until strawberries are starting to brown.
3. Remove from the oven and stir together with remaining sugar, lemon juice and mint. Macerate overnight in the fridge.
4. The next day, strain accumulated juices into a jam pot. Reserve berries. Boil juice to set at 220°F. Add berries and bring back to a boil, skimming often. Cook to set, again to 220°F; check set on a cold plate (see page 16).
5. Let sit 5 minutes, then ladle into hot sterilized jars, wipe rims, place sterilized lids on jars and process 10 to 15 minutes.

* You will need about 5¼ lb of whole fruit.

❧

GREAT WITH THE FOLLOWING RECIPES:
Toast Trio—Ricotta Toast, 117 | Ricotta & Jam Crostata, 206 | Roast Lamb & Moroccan Couscous, 177
PERFECT CHEESE PAIRING:
Gorgonzola
OTHER SERVING SUGGESTIONS:
Muddled into a mojito!

{YIELDS TEN TO TWELVE 8-OZ/250-ML JARS}

It seemed to take forever to get a significant crop from our sour cherry trees, but when they finally started producing fruit, it was a bumper, and so worth the wait! This Moroccan-spiced preserve was the first we created from the crop, and it quickly became one of our number-one sellers. Now we're back to wishing for more fruit. It might be time to find more yard space for a few extra trees!

MOROCCAN-SPICED SOUR CHERRY
— a Preservatory classic —

5 lb stemmed and pitted sour cherries*
4 lb (8 cups) sugar
¾ cup fresh lemon juice
3 tsp Moroccan Spice Mix (recipe opposite)

1. Combine all ingredients and macerate overnight in the fridge.
2. The next day, strain accumulated juices into a jam pot. Reserve cherries. Boil juice to set at 220°F. Add cherries and bring back to a boil, skimming often. Cook to set, again to 220°F; check set on a cold plate (see page 16).
3. Let sit 5 minutes, then ladle into hot sterilized jars, wipe rims, place sterilized lids on jars and process 10 to 15 minutes.

* You will need about 6 lb of whole fruit.

GREAT WITH THE FOLLOWING RECIPES:
Roast Lamb & Moroccan Couscous, 177 | Brandade Croquettes, 145 | Grilled Polenta & Blue Cheese, 155
PERFECT CHEESE PAIRING:
Pecorino
OTHER SERVING SUGGESTIONS:
In a pan sauce for duck | On cheesecake

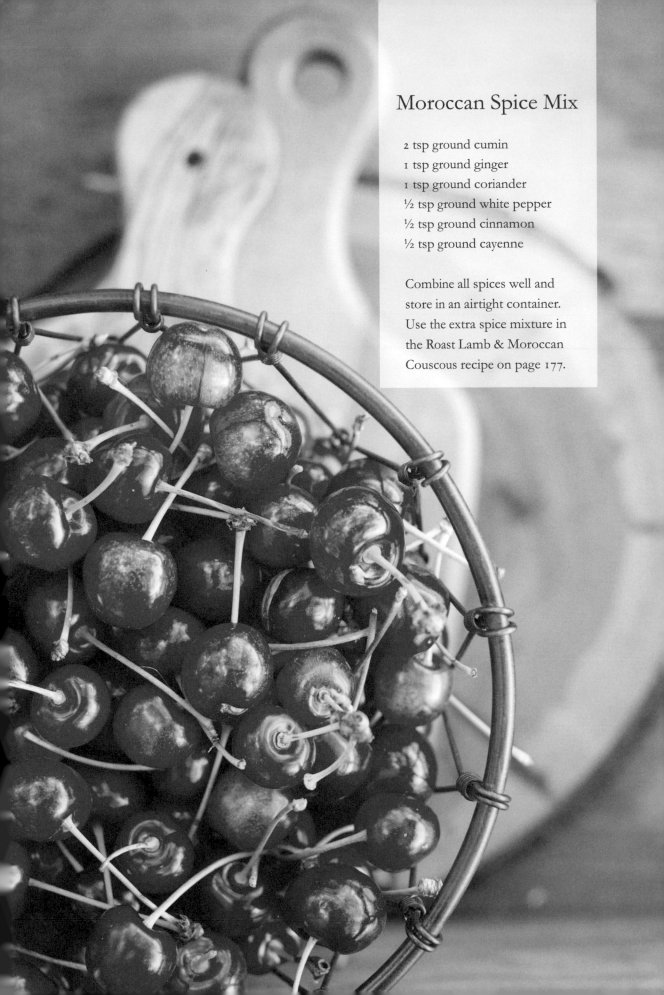

Moroccan Spice Mix

2 tsp ground cumin
1 tsp ground ginger
1 tsp ground coriander
½ tsp ground white pepper
½ tsp ground cinnamon
½ tsp ground cayenne

Combine all spices well and
store in an airtight container.
Use the extra spice mixture in
the Roast Lamb & Moroccan
Couscous recipe on page 177.

{YIELDS EIGHT TO TEN 8-OZ/250-ML JARS}

Rainier cherries, with their gorgeous yellow color, hint of red blush, and their delicate flavor, are my favorite of the cherry family. I like to use the cherries whole; however, you could chop them in a food processor first to make a more spreadable preserve. The addition of vanilla and kirsch is all that is needed to bring this preserve to its true calling—a sexy little preserve, if you will . . .

RAINIER CHERRY & KIRSCH

5 lb stemmed and pitted
   Rainier cherries or
   other sweet cherry*
1 vanilla bean

½ cup fresh lemon juice
4 lb (8 cups) sugar
⅓ cup + 1½ Tbsp kirsch

1. Cut vanilla bean in half lengthwise and scrape out the seeds with the dull side of a paring knife. Stir vanilla seeds into lemon juice and whisk to separate seeds.
2. Stir cherries together with sugar and vanilla-lemon juice. Macerate overnight in the fridge.
3. The next day, strain accumulated juices into a jam pot. Reserve cherries. Boil juice to set at 220°F, then add cherries and bring back to a boil, skimming often. Cook to set, again to 220°F; check set on a cold plate (see page 16).
4. Remove from heat and carefully stir in kirsch. Let sit 5 minutes, then, using slotted spoon, divide cherries evenly into sterilized jars. Top with cherry "syrup," wipe rims, place sterilized lids on jars and process 10 to 15 minutes.

* You will need about 6 lb of whole fruit.

GREAT WITH THE FOLLOWING RECIPES:
Bread Pudding with Chocolate & Jam, 213 | *Glazed Almond & Polenta Cake, 192* | *Best Crepes Ever! 128*
PERFECT CHEESE PAIRING:
Saint Agur or other creamy blue
OTHER SERVING SUGGESTIONS:
In the bottom of an Old-Fashioned cocktail | *On ice cream*

RASPBERRY WITH MERLOT &
PEPPERCORN

GREAT WITH THE FOLLOWING RECIPES:
Toast Trio—Ricotta Toast, 117
Chocolate Layer Cake, 198
Cheesecake Trio—Goat Cheese, 197
PERFECT CHEESE PAIRING:
Brillat-Savarin
OTHER SERVING SUGGESTIONS:
On chocolate ice cream | In a grilled cheese

RASPBERRY WITH CHOCOLATE & BRANDY

GREAT WITH THE FOLLOWING RECIPES:
Brie & Preserve–Stuffed French Toast, 120
Toast Trio—Spiced Walnut Butter Toast, 116 | Fritole, 200
OTHER SERVING SUGGESTIONS:
On chocolate cake | In muffin batter

Here's a little secret: if you're ever craving a spring jam in the middle of winter, frozen raspberries work beautifully. One of the only fruits that work as well from frozen as from fresh, raspberries have plenty of natural pectin, making raspberry preserves pretty fail-proof and quick to make. Our Raspberry with Merlot & Peppercorn preserve is one of our bestsellers—the not-too-subtle hint of peppercorn totally makes it. Raspberry with Chocolate & Brandy was another favorite in the test kitchen. Raspberries, chocolate and brandy are a match made in jam-making heaven.

RASPBERRY WITH MERLOT & PEPPERCORN
— *a Preservatory classic* —

5 lb raspberries
4 lb (8 cups) sugar
½ cup fresh lemon juice
½ cup Merlot
2 tsp cracked black peppercorns

1. If you're using fresh berries, give them a quick rinse if they need it.
2. Combine berries with the rest of the ingredients in a jam pot. Bring to a boil, stirring and skimming often. Cook jam to set at 220°F; check set on a cold plate (see page 16).
3. Let sit 5 minutes, then ladle into hot sterilized jars, wipe rims, place sterilized lids on jars and process 10 to 15 minutes.

RASPBERRY WITH CHOCOLATE & BRANDY

5 lb raspberries
4 lb (8 cups) sugar
½ cup fresh lemon juice
½ cup brandy
½ cup chopped dark chocolate

1. If you're using fresh berries, give them a quick rinse if they need it.
2. Combine berries with sugar and lemon juice in a jam pot. Bring to a boil, stirring and skimming often. Cook jam to set at 220°F; check set on a cold plate (see page 16).
3. Remove from heat and stir in brandy and chocolate to melt.
4. Let sit 5 minutes, then ladle into hot sterilized jars, wipe rims, place sterilized lids on jars and process 10 to 15 minutes.

{YIELDS TEN TO TWELVE 8-OZ/250-ML JARS}

I think it was the flowering French thyme blooming beside the greenhouse that had me thinking of this preserve. I'm very visual, and the lavender blue of the thyme flowers looked like a perfect match for blueberries. As it turns out, thankfully, it's also a delicious match! As blueberries have very little natural pectin, we process half the fruit to help reach the desired consistency.

BLUEBERRY & FRENCH THYME

5 lb blueberries	1 small bunch fresh thyme
4 lb (8 cups) sugar	(5 to 6 stems)
½ cup fresh lemon juice	Zest of 2 lemons

1. Rinse blueberries and process half in a food processor to a rough paste. Add to a jam pot with remaining ingredients.
2. Bring to a boil for 5 minutes. Cool and refrigerate overnight in the fridge.
3. The next day, bring back to a boil, stirring and skimming often. Cook jam to set at 220°F; check set on a cold plate (see page 16). Remove from heat and remove thyme stems.
4. Let sit 5 minutes, then ladle into hot sterilized jars, wipe rims, place sterilized lids on jars and process 10 to 15 minutes.

GREAT WITH THE FOLLOWING RECIPES:
Toast Trio—Ricotta Toast, 117 | Pan-Seared Duck Breast, 180
Glazed Almond & Polenta Cake, 192
PERFECT CHEESE PAIRING:
Saint Agur
OTHER SERVING SUGGESTIONS:
In cottage cheese | In a pan sauce for game meats

SUMMER

HAPPENING ON THE FARM

BBQs and green walnut harvest

IN SEASON

Tomatoes, apricots, peaches, plums, crabapples, blackberries, hardy herbs, corn and figs

Summer is fleeting in our growing region, lasting from mid-July to mid-September in a good year. The weather these last few years has really kept us guessing. We grow plums, tomatoes and crabapples on the farm. I guess you can count the blackberries, too—though they really grow themselves. The only thing we do is hack them back when they take over too much of the field.

Summer is also when we make our annual trek to the Okanagan Valley with family—which is crazy, because it's the busiest time of year at the farm and especially in the Preservatory. However, it's a 45-year-old tradition and such a welcome break in the middle of our busiest season, so we make it work no matter what. Getting to eat fresh, drippy peaches at their source makes it a pretty doable sacrifice—that and the Aperol spritzes from 11 a.m. on!

We eat easy in the Okanagan: a piece of meat on the grill, fresh no-cook tomato-sauce pasta with fresh-from-the-farm soft cheese. The produce at this time of year is so abundant, even the laziest cook can create a swoon-worthy meal without much time off the beach chair.

SUMMER PRESERVES

{YIELDS TWELVE TO FOURTEEN 8-OZ/250-ML JARS}

We source our apricots and other stone fruits from a wonderful organic family farm in the Similkameen Valley. It's such a treat to work with passionate farmers who take great pride in their crops. French tarragon is my favorite herb; its subtle licorice notes are a perfect match for the floral taste of the apricots. Tarragon is really the only herb that goes with almost everything. This preserve is so versatile; it does well in both sweet and savory dishes, though my favorite is with the Savory Dutch Baby (recipe page 130). So good!

APRICOT WITH TARRAGON & RIESLING
— a Preservatory classic —

5 lb halved and pitted apricots*
4 lb (8 cups) sugar
1 cup fresh lemon juice

1 cup spring water or distilled water
Small bunch fresh tarragon, 6 to 8 stems
½ cup Riesling

1. Stir together apricots, sugar, lemon juice, water and tarragon. Macerate overnight in the fridge.
2. The next day, combine mixture with Riesling in a jam pot and bring to a boil. Cook to set at 220°F; check set on a cold plate (see page 16). Remove from heat and remove tarragon stems.
3. Let sit 5 minutes, then ladle into hot sterilized jars, wipe rims, place sterilized lids on jars and process 10 to 15 minutes.

* You will need about 5¾ lb of whole fruit.

❧

GREAT WITH THE FOLLOWING RECIPES:
Coconut Curry Braised Chicken, 174 | Savory Dutch Baby, 130 | Ricotta & Jam Crostata, 206
PERFECT CHEESE PAIRING:
Bleu de Bresse
OTHER SERVING SUGGESTIONS:
On yogurt and granola | In muffin batter

Savory Dutch Baby, recipe page 130

{YIELDS TWELVE TO FOURTEEN 8-OZ/250-ML JARS}

Damson plums look a lot like their big sister, the Italian plum, yet they are so much more intense and a bit more sour. They make the best jam ever! The addition of sweet vermouth balances out the sour and makes a preserve that is as delicious as it is beautiful.

DAMSON PLUM & SWEET VERMOUTH

5 lb halved and pitted Damson plums or other tart plum*

1 vanilla bean

½ cup fresh lemon juice

4 lb (8 cups) sugar

½ cup sweet vermouth, red or white

1. Cut vanilla bean in half lengthwise and scrape out the seeds with the dull side of a paring knife. Stir vanilla seeds into lemon juice and whisk to separate seeds.
2. Combine plums, sugar and vanilla-lemon juice in a jam pot and bring to a boil. Remove from heat, cool and refrigerate overnight.
3. The next day, bring back to a boil and cook to 220°F; check set on a cold plate (see page 16).
4. Remove from heat and add vermouth. Stir and let sit 5 minutes, then ladle into hot sterilized jars, wipe rims, place sterilized lids on jars and process 10 to 15 minutes.

* You will need about 6 lb of whole fruit.

❧

GREAT WITH THE FOLLOWING RECIPES:
Toast Trio—Spiced Walnut Butter Toast, 116 | Brandade Croquettes, 145 | Delicious Pork Tenderloin, 173
PERFECT CHEESE PAIRING:
Piave Vecchio
OTHER SERVING SUGGESTIONS:
In a jelly roll | On a cheesecake

{YIELDS TWELVE TO FOURTEEN 8-OZ/250-ML JARS}

Our trips to Osoyoos in the sunny Okanagan involve bushels of peaches and grilling every evening, the inspiration for this sunny preserve. There's something glorious about grilled peaches. Grilling them heightens their sweet juiciness, and the note of smokiness adds complexity to the preserve. It's also way too hot for jammin' this time of year, and this extra step outdoors seemingly shortens the cooking time.

GRILLED PEACH WITH
BLACKBERRY & CANDIED GINGER

3 lb halved and pitted peaches*

2 Tbsp olive oil

2 lb blackberries, lightly rinsed
if needed

4 lb (8 cups) sugar

½ cup fresh lemon juice

½ lb candied ginger, finely chopped

1. Brush cut side of peach halves with olive oil and place on a hot grill. Grill just until you have nice dark grill marks, then remove, place in a bowl and cover with plastic wrap for 5 minutes; this will make removing the peach skins easier.
2. Peel peaches and chop. Combine grilled chopped peaches, blackberries, sugar, lemon juice and ginger in a jam pot and bring to a boil. Remove from heat, cool and refrigerate overnight.
3. The next day, bring back to a boil and cook to set at 220°F; check set on a cold plate (see page 16).
4. Remove from heat and let sit 5 minutes, then ladle into hot sterilized jars, wipe rims, place sterilized lids on jars and process 10 to 15 minutes.

* You will need about 4 lb of whole fruit.

❧

GREAT WITH THE FOLLOWING RECIPES:

Brie & Preserve–Stuffed French Toast, 120 | Crispy Pork Belly Bites, 147 | Queen of Puddings, 209

PERFECT CHEESE PAIRING:

Chèvre

OTHER SERVING SUGGESTIONS:

On a Pizzam base (page 185) with prawns | In sangria

{YIELDS TWELVE TO FOURTEEN 8-OZ/250-ML JARS}

Lemon verbena is one of my favorite herbs; a vaseful on your windowsill will scent your entire house with lemony floral loveliness for days! Sadly, we had to stop making this for a year when all my lemon verbena died in one of our harsher winters. Thankfully, we've now found a nearby farmer who has an abundant crop and is more than happy to share!

PEACH WITH
LEMON VERBENA & CHAMPAGNE
— a Preservatory classic —

5 lb peeled, pitted and chopped peaches*
4 lb (8 cups) sugar
½ cup fresh lemon juice
7 to 8 stems lemon verbena
½ cup champagne or Prosecco

1. Combine peaches, sugar and lemon juice in a jam pot. Bring to a boil over high heat.
2. Remove from heat and add lemon verbena, then cool and refrigerate overnight.
3. The next day, add champagne and bring back to a boil. Cook to set at 220°F; check set on a cold plate (see page 16).
4. Let sit 5 minutes, remove lemon verbena stems and as many leaves as possible, then ladle into hot sterilized jars, wipe rims, place sterilized lids on jars and process 10 to 15 minutes.

* You will need about 6½ lb of whole fruit.

❧

GREAT WITH THE FOLLOWING RECIPES:
Mum's Buttermilk Scones, 126 | Pan-Seared Duck Breast, 180 | Ricotta & Jam Crostata, 206
PERFECT CHEESE PAIRING:
Pecorino
OTHER SERVING SUGGESTIONS:
On scones | In Kir Preserve Royale, 234 (pictured opposite)

Early July is when we pick our walnuts, traditionally on Bastille Day. We harvest the walnuts while they are still green and considered a fruit. These get chopped and added to a local spirit, where they macerate until they are black and ready for fortifying our D'oro, a traditional French walnut wine. We then use the boozy walnuts to create our Green Walnut & Grappa preserve and the D'oro goes into our Figs & Walnut Wine preserve – our two bestselling preserves. They are a true zero waste crop for us.

{YIELDS TWELVE TO FOURTEEN 8-OZ/250-ML JARS}

I found it hard not to use this preserve as a suggestion for almost all of the recipes in Part II. It's so versatile, and the star anise puts it into its own category of deliciousness. It's gorgeous with cheese, with Spiced Walnut Butter (page 116) on a Pizzam (page 185), with Roast Lamb and Moroccan Couscous (page 177) . . . you get the idea. Make a batch or two; it won't last long! We use Italian plums for this, but any variety will do the trick.

PLUM WITH VANILLA & STAR ANISE
— *a Preservatory classic* —

5 lb halved and pitted plums*
4 lb (8 cups) sugar
½ cup fresh lemon juice
1 vanilla bean
8 whole star anise

1. Combine all ingredients in a jam pot and bring to a boil over high heat. Remove from heat, cool and refrigerate overnight.
2. The next day, bring back to a boil and cook to set at 220°F; check set on a cold plate (see page 16).
3. Remove star anise and let sit 5 minutes, then ladle into hot sterilized jars, wipe rims, place sterilized lids on jars and process 10 to 20 minutes.

* You will need about 6 lb of whole fruit.

❧

GREAT WITH THE FOLLOWING RECIPES:
Savory Dutch Baby, 130 | *Jam Tartlettes, 211* | *Duck Rillettes with Chive Cakes, 159*
PERFECT CHEESE PAIRING:
Cave-aged Gruyère
OTHER SERVING SUGGESTIONS:
On cheesecake | *In pan sauce*

{YIELDS TWELVE TO FOURTEEN 8-OZ/250-ML JARS}

Cultivated berries work for this preserve, but they taste nothing like the spicy deliciousness of the wild ones! I recommend long sleeves and gloves for harvesting. It's so much work, but so worth it! Only to be shared with loved ones . . .

PLAIN OL' WILD BLACKBERRY

5 lb blackberries, lightly rinsed if needed
4 lb (8 cups) sugar
½ cup fresh lemon juice

1. Stir together all ingredients in a jam pot and bring to a boil for 5 minutes. Cool and refrigerate overnight.
2. The next day, bring back to a boil, skimming often. Cook to set at 220°F; check set on a cold plate (see page 16).
3. Remove from heat, let sit 5 minutes, then ladle into hot sterilized jars, wipe rims, place sterilized lids on jars and process 10 to 20 minutes.

≈≈

GREAT WITH THE FOLLOWING RECIPES:
Grilled Polenta & Blue Cheese, 155 | *Eton Mess, 205* | *Grilled Wild Salmon, 170*
PERFECT CHEESE PAIRING:
Aged clothbound cheddar
OTHER SERVING SUGGESTIONS:
On pancakes | *In muffin batter*

{YIELDS TWELVE TO FOURTEEN 8-OZ/250-ML JARS}

You can use any variety of figs for this preserve. I used Brown Turkey figs, but Mission or Calimyrna would be just as lovely, or try combining a few different varieties if you can find them in season. I like to use a floral honey like wildflower, orange blossom or lavender. I would skip the star anise if you're using a floral honey so the latter can shine through!

FIG WITH HONEY & STAR ANISE

5 lb chopped fresh figs (remove tough ends of stems)*
4½ lb (6 cups) honey
½ cup fresh lemon juice
8 whole star anise

1. Combine all ingredients in a jam pot and bring to a boil over high heat. Remove from heat, cool and refrigerate overnight.
2. The next day, strain figs from the syrup and reserve. Bring syrup to a boil and cook to 220°F. Add figs to syrup and bring back to a boil. Cook to 220°F, then turn off heat and check set on a cold plate (see page 16).
3. Let sit 5 minutes, then ladle into hot sterilized jars, wipe rims, place sterilized lids on jars and process 10 to 15 minutes.

* You will need about 5¼ lb of whole fruit.

❦

GREAT WITH THE FOLLOWING RECIPES:
Cheesy Grits, 133 | *Cheesecake Trio—Blue Cheese, 197* | *Olive & Caramelized Onion Tart, 160*
PERFECT CHEESE PAIRING:
Any and all!
OTHER SERVING SUGGESTIONS:
On oatmeal | *In a layer cake*

Summertime and corn are a food memory that goes back to childhood—that and the butter-dish concave from rolling the cobs. A nice oaky, buttery Chardonnay takes the place of butter in this preserve, and it's a pretty great stand-in. Espelette pepper is slightly smoky, evoking the grilled corn cobs of summer backyard BBQs all year round, if you can make it last that long! My very punny son, Hunter, describes this jam as "ah-maizing!"

SWEET CORN WITH ESPELETTE & CHARDONNAY

5 lb fresh corn, cut off the cob
(if using frozen, simply thaw
and skip the first step)*
4 lb (8 cups) sugar
2 cups "Fresh" Apple Juice (page 21)

½ cup fresh lemon juice
½ cup Chardonnay
2 Tbsp Espelette pepper or
1 Tbsp smoked paprika
2 Tbsp smoked salt

1. Bring a pot of water to a boil. Boil corn for 1 minute, then drain.
2. Process half the corn in a food processor.
3. Combine mashed corn with remaining kernels, sugar, apple juice, lemon juice, Chardonnay and Espelette pepper in a jam pot. Bring to a boil over high heat. Cool and refrigerate overnight.
4. The next day, bring back to a boil and cook to set at 220°F; check set on a cold plate (see page 16). Stir in smoked salt.
5. Let sit 5 minutes, then ladle into hot sterilized jars, wipe rims, place sterilized lids on jars and process 10 to 20 minutes.

* You will need about 15 cobs.

GREAT WITH THE FOLLOWING RECIPES:
Brekkie Bowl, 125 | Grilled Flank Steak Salad, 167 | Grilled Polenta & Blue Cheese, 155
PERFECT CHEESE PAIRING:
Pecorino
OTHER SERVING SUGGESTIONS:
On corn tamales with salsa verde | In crab cakes

{YIELDS TWELVE TO FOURTEEN 8-OZ/250-ML JARS}

We started growing heirloom tomatoes in our greenhouse in 2001. It started innocently enough—about 5 varieties, 20 plants each—but then it became a bit of an obsession. At one point I had over 50 varieties in trays that held 100 seedlings—do the math . . . ri-dic-u-lous! Our greenhouse is about 500 square feet, tiny by farmer standards, so the tomatoes are started in the greenhouse before we move them out to the horses' riding ring, where they are staked in pots on the sand—a perfect growing environment, as it turns out! We still grow heirloom tomatoes, only these days in more realistic and manageable amounts.

HEIRLOOM TOMATO & CHILE
— a Preservatory classic —

5 lb cored and chopped heirloom tomatoes*
4 lb (8 cups) sugar
1 cup fresh lemon juice
2 Tbsp chile pepper flakes

1. Combine all ingredients in a jam pot. Bring to a boil for 5 minutes. Cool and refrigerate overnight.
2. The next day, bring mixture back to a boil over high heat. Cook to set at 220°F; check set on a cold plate (see page 16).
3. Let sit 5 minutes, then ladle into hot sterilized jars, wipe rims, place sterilized lids on jars and process 10 to 15 minutes.

* You will need about 5½ lb of whole tomatoes.

GREAT WITH THE FOLLOWING RECIPES:
Mama Ribs, 168 | Butter-BBQ'd Oysters, 148 | Hearty Skillet Hash, 141
PERFECT CHEESE PAIRING:
Mascarpone
OTHER SERVING SUGGESTIONS:
On Pizzam (page 185) | With cornbread

Almost as pretty as it tastes, this preserve was inspired by my favorite summer cocktail, the Aperol Spritz. We have a very old crabapple tree, at least 50 years old, on the property that produces a huge crop of the most beautiful tiny crabapples. For years, I hate to admit, we did nothing with them. We do now, and we've had to plant more crabapple trees to support the efforts of the older tree.

CRABAPPLE WITH ORANGE & APEROL

2 medium oranges
8 cups "Fresh" Crabapple Juice
(recipe below)

4 lb (8 cups) sugar
½ cup fresh lemon juice
½ cup Aperol

1. Slice oranges in half lengthwise, then very thinly slice and remove seeds.
2. Place all ingredients in a jam pot and bring to a boil over high heat, skimming and stirring often, as this one scorches easily. Cook to set at 220°F; check set on a cold plate (see page 16).
3. Let sit 5 minutes, then ladle into hot sterilized jars, wipe rims, place sterilized lids on jars and process 10 to 15 minutes.

{YIELDS TWELVE CUPS}

"Fresh" Crabapple Juice

5 ½ lb crabapples
4 cups water

1. Rinse and stem crabapples and cook in stockpot with water until very soft.
2. Pour into cheesecloth-lined sieve, pressing gently on mash to extract all the juice.
3. Freeze any leftover juice for later use. The frozen juice will keep for up to six months.

❧

GREAT WITH THE FOLLOWING RECIPES:
Glazed Country Ham & Jam-Baked Beans, 182 | *Glazed Almond & Polenta Cake, 192* | *Jam Tartlettes, 211*
PERFECT CHEESE PAIRING:
Manchego
OTHER SERVING SUGGESTIONS:
On rice pudding | *In Kir Preserve Royale, 234*

FALL

HAPPENING ON THE FARM

Grape harvest and non-stop production

IN SEASON

Apples, pears, peppers, cranberries, green tomatoes, tomatillos and veggies for pickling

Oh, fall—such a love-hate relationship we have. If you could just go a little slower with the fruit production at this time of year, we could get along so much better. Fall is when all the fruit on our farm seems to ripen on the same day—specifically apples and pears, our two largest crops—and, of course, the vineyard harvest usually coincides!

Fall is also when we have to harvest all the remaining tomatoes that haven't ripened, and in our climate there's usually a bumper crop of green tomatoes. And fall is pickle season, so I decided to create a new lineup of fun flavors—you know, 'cause we had nothing else to do at this time of year!

The love is for the gorgeous weather that typically defines fall in our area. We live across from Campbell Valley Regional Park, which in September and October is a riot of color from the changing leaves. I'm also a Libra, which makes the fall even more special to me . . . even if it means getting another year older.

FALL PRESERVES

{YIELDS TWELVE TO FOURTEEN 8-OZ/250-ML JARS}

This preserve was made with my Grandma Gracie hovering over my shoulder, at least in spirit. I can see her slightly burnt toast with lots of soft butter and this preserve heaped on.

NOTE: Though the addition of bacon is awesome, for safety's sake, we store this preserve in the fridge after it cools. Unopened it will last 3 months; once opened, use within 10 days.

HERITAGE APPLE
WITH BACON & SCOTCH
— a Preservatory classic —

4½ lb peeled, cored and chopped
  apples, heritage or otherwise*
4 lb (8 cups) sugar
1 cup fresh lemon juice

1 Tbsp coarsely ground pepper
½ lb crisply cooked bacon, chopped fine
½ cup Scotch

1. Stir apples together with sugar, lemon juice and pepper in a jam pot. Bring to a boil. Cool and refrigerate overnight.
2. The next day, cook and chop bacon. Add to mixture and bring back to a boil, to 220°F, skimming often. Check set on a cold plate (see page 16).
3. Remove from heat and carefully pour in Scotch—it will bubble up, so be careful!
4. Stir and let sit 5 minutes, then ladle into hot sterilized jars, wipe rims, place sterilized lids on jars, cool and refrigerate. See note above.

* You will need about 6 lb of whole fruit.

❧

GREAT WITH THE FOLLOWING RECIPES:
Brûléed Steel-Cut Oatmeal, 119 | Crispy Pork Belly Bites, 147 | Buttermilk Panna Cotta, 195
PERFECT CHEESE PAIRING:
Smoked Gouda
OTHER SERVING SUGGESTIONS:
On oatcakes, pictured opposite | In a grilled cheese

{YIELDS TWELVE TO FOURTEEN 8-OZ/250-ML JARS}

Pears are my favorite fruit. I'm terrible at getting my daily intake of fresh fruit unless it's pear season, and then I totally make up for the rest of the year. I actually find it hard to fill the jam pot, as I'm constantly stealing bits. Don't let the simple nature of this preserve deter you from trying it. The subtle addition of vanilla truly makes the pear shine.

PEAR & VANILLA BEAN
— a Preservatory classic —

5 lb peeled, cored and thinly sliced pears*
1 vanilla bean
½ cup fresh lemon juice
4 lb (8 cups) sugar

1. Cut vanilla bean in half lengthwise and scrape out seeds with the dull side of a paring knife. Stir vanilla seeds into lemon juice and whisk to separate seeds.
2. Stir sliced pears together with sugar and vanilla-lemon juice in a jam pot. Bring to a boil for 5 minutes. Cool and refrigerate overnight.
3. The next day, bring mixture back to a boil, skimming often. Cook to set, again to 220°F; check set on a cold plate (see page 16).
4. Remove from heat and let sit 5 minutes, then ladle into hot sterilized jars, wipe rims, place sterilized lids on jars and process 10 to 15 minutes.

* You will need about 6 lb of whole fruit.

❧

GREAT WITH THE FOLLOWING RECIPES:
Carrot Cake Waffles, 134 | *Queen of Puddings, 209* | *Mum's Buttermilk Scones, 126*
PERFECT CHEESE PAIRING:
Brie
OTHER SERVING SUGGESTIONS:
On hot buttered toast | *In a martini*

{YIELDS TWELVE TO FOURTEEN 8-OZ/250-ML JARS}

All the amazing pear and chocolate desserts I've inhaled in Paris are the inspirations behind this recipe. One of my favorite flavor combinations, this preserve is complete heaven on a warm, flaky croissant!

PEAR & COCOA NIB
— a Preservatory classic —

5 lb peeled, cored and chopped pears*
4 lb (8 cups) sugar
½ cup fresh lemon juice
¼ cup cocoa nibs (available at specialty grocers)

1. Combine chopped pears with sugar and lemon juice in a jam pot and bring just to a boil. Cool and refrigerate overnight.
2. The next day, bring mixture back to a boil, skimming often. Cook to set at 220°F; check set on a cold plate (see page 16). Remove from heat and stir in cocoa nibs.
3. Let sit 5 minutes, then ladle into hot sterilized jars, wipe rims, place sterilized lids on jars and process 10 to 15 minutes.

* You will need about 6 lb of whole fruit.

❧

GREAT WITH THE FOLLOWING RECIPES:
Bruléed Steel-Cut Oatmeal, 119 | Nutty Ricotta Jamcakes, 136 | Fritole, 200
PERFECT CHEESE PAIRING:
Mascarpone
OTHER SERVING SUGGESTIONS:
On that warm croissant mentioned above | In crepes

{YIELDS TWELVE TO FOURTEEN 8-OZ/250-ML JARS}

This one may seem a little crazy. The idea originally came to me during a meal at the beautiful Stone Barns farm in upstate New York. The most memorable dish of the night was a beet jam and foie gras terrine. It was totally over the top and completely unexpected, with a texture similar to peanut butter and jelly. Weird and wonderful, like this preserve!

BEET WITH
ORANGES & PINK PEPPERCORN
— a Preservatory classic —

5 lb beets*
4 lb (8 cups) sugar
⅔ cup fresh lemon juice
Zest of 2 medium oranges
½ cup fresh orange juice
2 Tbsp pink peppercorns, crushed

1. Boil beets until tender, about 20 to 30 minutes. Cool slightly, then peel and process in a food processor until finely minced.
2. Combine all ingredients in a jam pot and bring to a boil over high heat, stirring often. Be careful, this one is a splurter! Cook to set at 220°F; check set on a cold plate (see page 16).
3. Let sit 5 minutes, then ladle into hot sterilized jars, wipe rims, place sterilized lids on jars and process 15 to 20 minutes.

* You will need about 5 ½ lb of whole beets.

❧

GREAT WITH THE FOLLOWING RECIPES:
Brekkie Bowl, 125 | Grilled Polenta & Blue Cheese, 155 | Grilled Flank Steak Salad, 167
PERFECT CHEESE PAIRING:
Chèvre
OTHER SERVING SUGGESTIONS:
On crostini with mint | In a pan sauce for duck

{YIELDS TWELVE TO FOURTEEN 8-OZ/250-ML JARS}

This is what happens when I let my husband, Patrick, loose with the seed catalogue: we had more than 30 varieties of peppers one year. Not knowing what each pepper's "hot" factor was, and too much of a wimp to taste them raw, I threw them all in the processor and crossed my fingers. BEST jam ever! Base your own assortment on how much heat you can handle, or go the surprise route like I did!

N O T E : Wear disposable gloves when handling hot peppers. Trust me, one night of sleeping with your hands in buttermilk and you'll always remember this!

CHILE PEPPER
— a Preservatory classic —

5 lb halved and seeded assorted peppers (jalapeño, serrano, sweet bell, pepperoncini, Anaheim, etc.), stem and pith removed*

4 lb (8 cups) sugar
4 cups "Fresh" Apple Juice (page 21)
1 cup fresh lemon juice

1. Pulse peppers in a food processor until finely chopped.
2. Combine all ingredients in a jam pot and bring to a boil over high heat. Remove from heat, cool and refrigerate overnight.
3. The next day, bring back to a boil and cook to set at 220°F; check set on a cold plate (see page 16).
4. Let sit 5 minutes, then ladle into hot sterilized jars, wipe rims, place sterilized lids on jars and process 10 to 15 minutes.

* You will need about 5¾ lb of whole peppers.

GREAT WITH THE FOLLOWING RECIPES:
Mama Ribs, 168 | Indian-Spiced Lamb Balls, 156 | Brandade Croquettes, 145
PERFECT CHEESE PAIRING:
Ricotta
OTHER SERVING SUGGESTIONS:
On a fried egg sandwich, pictured opposite | In quesadillas

{YIELDS FOURTEEN TO SIXTEEN 8-OZ/250-ML JARS}

If you're a fan of sweet potato pie, add this preserve to your repertoire. The candied pecans are optional, but add nice texture and crunch. This preserve is great to have on hand for an easy last-minute dessert; just fill a tart crust with this preserve and you're golden!

SWEET POTATO PIE

5 lb peeled and cubed sweet potatoes*
4½ lb (9 cups) sugar
2 cups "Fresh" Apple Juice (page 21)
1 cup fresh lemon juice
3 tsp ground cinnamon
2 whole nutmeg, grated
½ cup chopped Easy Candied Pecans (page 137)

1. Boil sweet potatoes about 20 to 30 minutes until very soft. Drain well and mash.
2. Combine mashed sweet potatoes, sugar, apple juice, lemon juice and spices in a jam pot. Bring to a boil. Stir constantly, as this one has a tendency to stick! Cook to set at 220°F; check set on a cold plate (see page 16). Stir in chopped pecans.
3. Let sit 5 minutes, then ladle into hot sterilized jars, wipe rims, place sterilized lids on jars and process 15 to 20 minutes.

* You will need about 5 ½ lb of whole sweet potatoes.

GREAT WITH THE FOLLOWING RECIPES:
Hearty Skillet Hash, 141 | *Fritole, 200* | *Jam Tartlettes sprinkled with extra candied pecans, 211*
PERFECT CHEESE PAIRING:
Gorgonzola
OTHER SERVING SUGGESTIONS:
On meatloaf | In muffin batter

{YIELDS FOURTEEN TO SIXTEEN 8-OZ/250-ML JARS}

You'll want to keep a few jars of this preserve on hand for easy last-minute appetizers. This versatile condiment is great with cheeses, with grilled meats or in stir-fries. Don't cook this one in copper; it has too much acid from the vinegar, which will react with copper and leach unwanted metal into the preserves.

SPICY SWEET CHARRED ONION & FIGS

5 lb sweet onions, sliced thin

2¾ lb (4¾ cups) demerara sugar
   or brown sugar

2½ lb dried figs, chopped

2 cups sherry vinegar

2 Tbsp Szechuan peppercorns, crushed

1. Preheat oven to 425°F.

2. Lay out onion slices on parchment-lined baking sheets and sprinkle evenly with some of the sugar, reserving the remainder for the following step. Bake for 10 minutes, then broil for an additional 3 to 5 minutes to get a nice char.

3. Combine all ingredients in a large saucepan (not copper!). Bring to a boil over medium-high heat, then reduce to medium-low, stirring often at the beginning. When liquid begins to reduce, stir continuously to avoid scorching. Cook until thick and of jam-like consistency.

4. Let sit 5 minutes, then ladle into hot sterilized jars, wipe rims, place sterilized lids on jars and process 15 to 20 minutes.

∾

GREAT WITH THE FOLLOWING RECIPES:

Hearty Skillet Hash, 141 | *Grilled Flank Steak Salad, 167* | *Olive & Caramelized Onion Tart, 160*

PERFECT CHEESE PAIRING:

Saint Agur

OTHER SERVING SUGGESTIONS:

On a charcuterie board | *In a burger*

If there is a better way to use the unripened tomato harvest than this preserve, I haven't found it. Sure, fried green tomatoes are unreal—so good—but after the third day, the guilt is unbearable. This is a much more sustainable application and one that will see you well into the winter. This preserve is so versatile—sweet but with so much depth of flavor—that I guarantee you'll find more uses than you'll have enough jars for.

INDIAN-SPICED GREEN TOMATO

2 tsp fenugreek
1 tsp nigella/kalonji seeds
10 dried curry leaves
½ tsp ground cardamom

5 lb cored and chopped
  green (unripe) tomatoes*
4 lb (8 cups) sugar
½ cup fresh lemon juice

1. Using a spice grinder or a mortar and pestle, grind fenugreek, nigella and curry leaves to a fine powder. Stir ground cardamom into mixture.
2. Combine green tomatoes, sugar, lemon juice and ground spices in a jam pot and bring to a boil over high heat. Remove from heat, cool and refrigerate overnight.
3. The next day, bring back to a boil and cook to set at 220°F; check set on a cold plate (see page 16).
4. Let sit 5 minutes, then ladle into hot sterilized jars, wipe rims, place sterilized lids on jars and process 15 to 20 minutes.

* You will need about 5½ lb of whole tomatoes.

෨෬

GREAT WITH THE FOLLOWING RECIPES:
Indian-Spiced Lamb Balls, 156 | *Crispy Pork Belly Bites, 147* | *Coconut Curry Braised Chicken, 174*
PERFECT CHEESE PAIRING:
Cave-aged Gruyère
OTHER SERVING SUGGESTIONS:
On a fried egg | *In curries*

Once, while I was searching for tamarillos, an exotic red tree fruit, at Granville Island here in Vancouver, the lovely shopkeeper first brought me turmeric, then tomatillos. After much giggling, we determined she did not have tamarillos. I continued my shopping, and when I got to the till, she said, "I thought you didn't want the tomatillos." I didn't, but by this time I'd created a new preserve in my head and now NEEDED the tomatillos. Okay, maybe this was funnier at the time!

TOMATILLO & CHILE

5 lb washed, cored and chopped tomatillos*

4 lb (8 cups) sugar

½ cup fresh lemon juice

2 poblano peppers, pith and seeds removed, chopped

4 red chile peppers, pith and seeds removed, chopped

2 habanero peppers, pith and seeds removed, chopped

1 Tbsp coriander seeds, crushed

1. Combine tomatillos, sugar, lemon juice, chopped peppers and coriander in a jam pot and bring to a boil. Remove from heat, cool and refrigerate overnight.
2. The next day, bring back to a boil and cook at 220°F; check set on a cold plate (see page 16).
3. Let sit 5 minutes, then ladle into hot sterilized jars, wipe rims, place sterilized lids on jars and process 15 to 20 minutes.

* You will need about 5 ½ lb of whole tomatillos.

❧

GREAT WITH THE FOLLOWING RECIPES:
Toast Trio—Avocado Toast, 116 | Butter-BBQ'd Oysters, 148 | Coconut Curry Braised Chicken, 174
PERFECT CHEESE PAIRING:
Queso fresco
OTHER SERVING SUGGESTIONS:
On rare tuna | In tacos

Olive & Caramelized Onion Tart, recipe page 160

{YIELDS TWELVE TO FOURTEEN 8-OZ/250-ML JARS}

I use Kalamata olives for this curious preserve, but any mix of brine-packed olives will work as beautifully. "Weirdly wonderful," as described by one taste tester, this preserve was inspired by all the Mediterranean flavors I love and brings to mind lazy afternoons and delicious aperitivo.

OLIVE WITH ORANGE & LEMON

5 lb pitted olives

4 lb (8 cups) sugar

2 cups "Fresh" Apple Juice (page 21)

Zest of 2 lemons

2 cups fresh lemon juice

Zest of 2 medium oranges

2 to 3 stems fresh rosemary

4 to 5 stems fresh thyme

1. Pulse olives in a food processor until finely chopped.
2. Combine all ingredients in a jam pot and bring to a boil. Remove from heat, cool and refrigerate overnight.
3. The next day, bring back to a boil and cook to set at 220°F; check set on a cold plate (see page 16).
4. Remove rosemary and thyme stems and let sit 5 minutes, then ladle into hot sterilized jars, wipe rims, place sterilized lids on jars and process 15 to 20 minutes.

❧

GREAT WITH THE FOLLOWING RECIPES:

Brekkie Bowl, 125 | Brandade Croquettes, 145 | Olive & Caramelized Onion Tart (pictured), 160

PERFECT CHEESE PAIRING:

Pecorino

OTHER SERVING SUGGESTIONS:

On baked chicken | In vinaigrette (see page 122)

WINTER

HAPPENING ON THE FARM

Cookies for Kids and family snow days

IN SEASON

Citrus, mango, pineapple, bananas, persimmon

We do a fundraiser at the farm every Christmas which we call Cookies for Kids. We began the endeavor in 2005 and to date have raised over $90,000 for BC Children's Hospital. We combine delicious cookie donations from some of Vancouver's best chefs and bakers with a jar of our preserves in red cookie tins, which are sold by donation. We do it in honor of Patrick's sister and my cousin, both Teresas, both lost too young. Our wish is to make Christmas a little sweeter for everyone in their memory.

We're blessed with a very mild climate here in South Langley; we rarely see snow, and when we do it's usually short-lived. We are, however, only a couple of hours away from Whistler, and even closer to our local ski hills. While we don't get up to the mountains as much as we did when we could still keep up with the kids, we do try to do a few family trips each season. I love these trips: family time, cozy comfort foods and hot toddies!

Winter may be when the farm is at rest, but the Preservatory keeps humming along as we bring in the citrus and other tropical fruits to keep the pots hot.

WINTER PRESERVES

Duck Rillettes with Chive Cakes, recipe page 159

{YIELDS TWELVE TO FOURTEEN 8-OZ/250-ML JARS}

This preserve was one of our first and is still one of my favorites. The only reason we don't produce it commercially anymore is a mutiny at the Preservatory prep table! Kumquats are a pain in the butt; however, the rewards are well worth the effort. Try this preserve in the bottom of a vodka martini—trust me!

KUMQUAT WITH VANILLA & VODKA

5 lb sliced, seeded kumquats*
1 vanilla bean
½ cup fresh lemon juice
4½ lb (9 cups) sugar
2 cups fresh orange juice
½ cup vanilla vodka

1. Cut vanilla bean in half lengthwise and scrape out seeds with the dull side of a paring knife. Stir seeds into lemon juice and whisk to separate seeds.
2. Stir sliced kumquats together with sugar, vanilla-lemon juice and orange juice in a jam pot. Bring to a boil for 5 minutes. Cool and refrigerate overnight.
3. The next day, bring back to a boil, skimming often. Cook to 218°F, add vodka off heat, then return to heat and bring back to a boil. Cook to set at 220°F; check set on a cold plate (see page 16).
4. Remove from heat and let sit 5 minutes, then ladle into hot sterilized jars, wipe rims, place hot sterilized lids on jars and process 10 to 15 minutes.

* You will need about 5½ lb of whole fruit.

❧

GREAT WITH THE FOLLOWING RECIPES:
Duck Rillettes with Chive Cakes, 159 | *Glazed Almond & Polenta Cake, 192*
Brie & Preserve–Stuffed French Toast, 120
PERFECT CHEESE PAIRING:
Saint-André
OTHER SERVING SUGGESTIONS:
On cheesecake | *In a martini*

{YIELDS TEN TO TWELVE 8-OZ/250-ML JARS}

We made this preserve for years, and I'm pretty sure it'll be back in circulation now that we've dusted off the recipe. This makes the best grown-up PB&Js! You'll want to use nearly ripe bananas for this—too ripe and you'll have a mashed mess. A little green at the stem is perfect.

BANANA WITH PASSION FRUIT & RUM

3 lb peeled and sliced banana*
1 cup passion fruit purée (available in the freezer section of specialty grocers)

3½ lb (7 cups) sugar
1 cup fresh lemon juice
½ cup rum

1. Combine banana slices, passion fruit purée, sugar and lemon juice in a jam pot. Bring to a boil, stirring and skimming often. Be careful; this one can scorch and splatter a bit. Cook jam to set at 220°F; check set on a cold plate (see page 16).
2. Remove from heat and stir in rum. Let sit 5 minutes, then ladle into hot sterilized jars, wipe rims, place sterilized lids on jars and process 10 to 15 minutes.

* You will need about 4½ lb of whole bananas.

GREAT WITH THE FOLLOWING RECIPES:
Brûléed Steel-Cut Oatmeal, 119 | *Bread Pudding with Chocolate & Jam, 213* | *Carrot Cake Waffles, 134*
PERFECT CHEESE PAIRING:
Ricotta
OTHER SERVING SUGGESTIONS:
On peanut butter sandwiches | *In crepes*

{YIELDS FOURTEEN TO SIXTEEN 8-OZ/250-ML JARS}

Here's another blast from the past. We made this for only a couple of years, and I'm not sure why it isn't still in production. Pretty sure we'll be remedying that this winter! This is like Christmas pudding in a jar. It's decadent over ice cream but versatile enough to pair with a lovely bit of beef tenderloin for a truly unique crostini.

CHESTNUT WITH DATES & BRANDY

2½ lb canned whole chestnuts, drained, rinsed and chopped

2½ lb pitted and chopped dates

4½ lb (9 cups) sugar

1 cup fresh lemon juice

4 cups water

2 tsp cinnamon

½ cup brandy

1. Combine chestnuts, dates, sugar, lemon juice, water and cinnamon in a jam pot. Bring to a boil, stirring and skimming often. Cook jam to set at 220°F; check set on a cold plate (see page 16).

2. Remove from heat and stir in brandy.

3. Let sit 5 minutes, then ladle into hot sterilized jars, wipe rims, place sterilized lids on jars and process 10 to 20 minutes.

GREAT WITH THE FOLLOWING RECIPES:

Brandade Croquettes, 145 | Delicious Pork Tenderloin, 173 | Bread Pudding with Chocolate & Jam, 213

PERFECT CHEESE PAIRING:

Comté

OTHER SERVING SUGGESTIONS:

On beef tenderloin crostini with horseradish cream | In a tart shell

{YIELDS TWELVE TO FOURTEEN 8-OZ/250-ML JARS}

I *love* Lillet. If you've never tried it, I recommend picking up a bottle of this lovely French aperitif. Try it simply on the rocks and then get to work on this preserve. Lillet Blanc has a distinct orange flavor, and this preserve, with the tart blood orange and the coconut bringing an exotic smoothness to round out the flavors, is my new favorite. I may have already said this, but I mean it this time!

BLOOD ORANGE WITH COCONUT & LILLET

15 blood oranges
1 vanilla bean
4 lb (8 cups) sugar
4 cups "Fresh" Apple Juice (page 21)

½ cup fresh lemon juice
1 cup unsweetened shredded coconut
½ cup Lillet Blanc

1. Zest all of the blood oranges. Juice half and peel and segment the other half. Combined, you should have 4½ lb of zest, juice and orange segments.
2. Cut vanilla bean in half lengthwise and scrape out vanilla seeds with the dull side of a paring knife. Stir seeds into lemon juice and whisk to separate seeds.
3. Combine blood orange juice, zest and segments with sugar, apple juice and vanilla-lemon juice in a jam pot. Bring to a boil for 5 minutes. Cool and refrigerate overnight.
4. The next day, bring back to a boil, skimming often. Cook to 218°F. Add coconut and Lillet Blanc off heat, then return to heat and bring back to a boil. Cook to set at 220°F; check set on a cold plate (see page 16).
5. Remove from heat and let sit 5 minutes, then ladle into hot sterilized jars, wipe rims, place sterilized lids on jars and process 10 to 15 minutes.

❧

GREAT WITH THE FOLLOWING RECIPES:
Glazed Almond & Polenta Cake, 192 | *Duck Rillettes with Chive Cakes, 159* | *Mum's Buttermilk Scones, 126*
PERFECT CHEESE PAIRING:
Comté
OTHER SERVING SUGGESTIONS:
On cheesecake | *In a jelly roll*

{YIELDS FOURTEEN TO SIXTEEN 8-OZ/250-ML JARS}

This preserve smells like Christmas and tastes like it too! It's perfect for gifting at the holidays. It's gorgeous as a glaze for your holiday ham and of course as a base for a non-traditional hot mulled wine.

MULLED WINE JELLY

5 whole star anise

12 whole cardamom pods

1 tsp whole peppercorns

1 tsp whole allspice

3 sticks cinnamon, broken in half

¼ tsp whole cloves

1 whole nutmeg, grated

8 cups "Fresh" Apple Juice (page 21)

8 cups red wine

4½ lb (9 cups) sugar

½ cup fresh lemon juice

Zest and juice of 2 medium oranges

1. Place all spices in cheesecloth and tie with kitchen twine. Add to a jam pot with remaining ingredients and bring to a boil for 5 minutes. Cool and refrigerate overnight.

2. The next day, bring back to a boil, skimming often. Cook to set at 220°F; check set on a cold plate (see page 16). Remove from heat and carefully remove spices.

3. Let sit 5 minutes, then ladle into hot sterilized jars, wipe rims, place sterilized lids on jars and process 10 to 15 minutes.

❧

GREAT WITH THE FOLLOWING RECIPES:

Glazed Chicken Drummettes, 163 | *Duck Rillettes with Chive Cakes, 159*

Glazed Country Ham & Jam-Baked Beans, 182

PERFECT CHEESE PAIRING:

Parmigiano-Reggiano

OTHER SERVING SUGGESTIONS:

On ice cream | *In Vista D'oro Mulled Wine (page 240)*

{YIELDS FOURTEEN TO SIXTEEN 8-OZ/250-ML JARS}

I had always planned to create a full cocktail line of preserves. It hasn't happened yet, but I'm sure it will one day soon. In the meantime, here's one inspired by one of the first preserves I remember making with my mum. I think it was actually a strawberry daiquiri freezer jam with rum. This is the more mature version.

SMOKED LIME MARGARITA

6 limes

5 lb (10 cups) sugar, divided

2 cups water

3 cups "Fresh" Apple Juice (page 21)

½ cup fresh lemon juice

2 Tbsp flaked smoked salt

½ cup tequila

1. Rinse limes and cut in half lengthwise, then slice very thinly.
2. Combine lime slices with 1 lb (2 cups) of the sugar and the water in a jam pot. Bring to a simmer and poach limes until very soft and translucent.
3. Add apple juice, lemon juice and the remaining sugar and bring to a boil for 5 minutes. Cool and refrigerate overnight.
4. The next day, bring back to a boil and cook to set at 220°F; check set on a cold plate (see page 16). Off heat, gently stir in smoked salt and tequila, then bring back to one last boil.
5. Let sit 5 minutes, then ladle into hot sterilized jars, wipe rims, place sterilized lids on jars and process 10 to 15 minutes.

❧

GREAT WITH THE FOLLOWING RECIPES:
Coconut Curry Braised Chicken, 174 | *Glazed Almond & Polenta Cake, 192* | *Jamargaritas, 233*
PERFECT CHEESE PAIRING:
Queso fresco
OTHER SERVING SUGGESTIONS:
On panna cotta | *In a stir-fry*

Pineapples are beginning to take over the copper pots at the Preservatory during the winter months, and I couldn't be happier. The fresh tropical sweetness brightens the cold, drizzly days here on the "wet" coast. The Piña Colada preserve is seriously good! Our crew came up with about a million things to slather this on: crab cakes, coconut-crusted chicken, prawns, ice cream sundaes, pancakes . . . well, maybe not a million, but you get this gist. Not to be outdone, the Pineapple with Mint & Chile is another new favorite. The fresh pineapple flavor with a hint of heat is the perfect condiment for so many recipes. I've even mixed it with some hot mustard and topped a hot dog in a moment of weakness . . . so good!

PIÑA COLADA

5 lb peeled and chopped pineapple*
4 lb (8 cups) sugar
¾ cup fresh lemon juice
1 cup coconut water
1 cup unsweetened shredded coconut
½ cup rum

1. Stir together chopped pineapple, sugar, lemon juice and coconut water in a jam pot and bring to a boil for 5 minutes. Cool and refrigerate overnight.
2. The next day, bring back to a boil and cook to set at 220°F; check set on a cold plate (see page 16). Remove from heat and stir in coconut and carefully add the rum, as it may cause the hot jam to splatter.
3. Let sit 5 minutes, then ladle into hot sterilized jars, wipe rims, place sterilized lids on jars and process 10 to 15 minutes.

PINEAPPLE WITH MINT & CHILE

5 lb peeled and chopped pineapple*
4 lb (8 cups) sugar
¾ cup fresh lemon juice
½ cup chopped fresh mint
6 to 12 whole dried chile peppers

1. Stir together all ingredients in a jam pot and bring to a boil for 5 minutes. Cool and refrigerate overnight.
2. The next day, bring back to a boil and cook to set at 220°F; check set on a cold plate (see page 16). Remove from heat, remove chiles (see note) and stir.
3. Let sit 5 minutes, then ladle into hot sterilized jars, wipe rims, place sterilized lids on jars and process 10 to 15 minutes.

NOTE: For a little extra heat and pretty presentation, leave in the whole chiles, dividing evenly between jars.

* You will need about 6 to 7 whole pineapples for each recipe.

PIÑA COLADA

GREAT WITH THE FOLLOWING RECIPES:

Carrot Cake Waffles, 134 | *Chocolate Layer Cake, 198* | *Eton Mess, 205*

PERFECT CHEESE PAIRING:

Ricotta

OTHER SERVING SUGGESTIONS:

On crab cakes | *In yogurt granola parfait*

PINEAPPLE WITH MINT & CHILE (pictured)

GREAT WITH THE FOLLOWING RECIPES:

Crispy Pork Belly Bites, 147 | *Indian-Spiced Lamb Balls, 156* | *Grilled Wild Salmon, 170*

PERFECT CHEESE PAIRING:

Queso fresco

OTHER SERVING SUGGESTIONS:

On Pizzams, 185 | *In fish tacos*

Persimmons are one of those fruits you see in the market and wonder about—at least they were for me. Now that we've played with them in the Preservatory, I can't wait to create more with this beautiful fruit. Their glowing red-orange color is gorgeous, and they have a very delicate honey-like flavor.

PERSIMMON WITH CINNAMON & PECANS

5 lb cored, firm persimmons*
4 lb (8 cups) sugar
½ cup fresh lemon juice

2 sticks cinnamon
1 cup chopped Easy Candied Pecans
(page 137)

1. Pulse persimmons in a food processor until finely chopped.
2. Combine chopped persimmons, sugar, lemon juice and cinnamon sticks in a jam pot. Bring to a boil for 5 minutes. Remove from heat, cool and refrigerate overnight.
3. The next day, bring back to a boil, stirring often, and cook to 220°F; check set on a cold plate (see page 16).
4. Remove cinnamon sticks. Stir in chopped pecans and let sit 5 minutes, then ladle into hot sterilized jars, wipe rims, place sterilized lids on jars and process 15 to 20 minutes.

* You will need about 5½ lb of whole fruit.

❧

GREAT WITH THE FOLLOWING RECIPES:
Fritole, 200 | Nutty Ricotta Jamcakes, 136 | Roast Lamb & Moroccan Couscous, 177
PERFECT CHEESE PAIRING:
Münster
OTHER SERVING SUGGESTIONS:
On baked ham | In muffin batter

{YIELDS TWELVE TO FOURTEEN 8-OZ/250-ML JARS}

Here's another fan favorite from the archives, this one a very British preserve—or marmalade, really. Seville oranges are very short-seasoned and fleeting in the market, and there really is no substitute for these bitter beauties. When you see them, grab them! A true labor of love, this preserve takes a wee bit of time to make, but it is so lovely on a buttermilk scone with a cup of tea in the afternoon, you'll be glad you did.

SEVILLE ORANGE
WITH CARDAMOM & BRANDY
— a Preservatory classic —

30 Seville oranges

1 cup fresh lemon juice

4½ lb (9 cups) sugar

⅓ cup whole cardamom pods

½ cup brandy

1. Peel zest from oranges using a potato peeler, being careful not to get any of the white pith, then thinly slice the peel.

2. Bring the orange peel to a boil in water to cover. Drain and boil again in fresh water. Drain and reserve water.

3. Juice the oranges. Combine orange juice, lemon juice, sugar and cardamom pods in a jam pot. Bring to a simmer for 5 minutes, then add reserved zest with water and bring to a boil for 10 more minutes to reduce. Cool and refrigerate overnight.

4. The next day, bring back to a boil, skimming often. Cook to set at 220°F; check set on a cold plate (see page 16). Remove from heat, remove cardamom pods and carefully stir in brandy.

5. Let sit 5 minutes, then ladle into hot sterilized jars, wipe rims, place sterilized lids on jars and process 10 to 15 minutes.

❧

GREAT WITH THE FOLLOWING RECIPES:
Delicious Pork Tenderloin, 173 | Mama Ribs, 168 | Ricotta & Jam Crostata, 206
PERFECT CHEESE PAIRING:
Crottin de Chavignol
OTHER SERVING SUGGESTIONS:
In hot tea | On scones

Ricotta & Jam Crostata, recipe page 206

PART II

RECIPES WITH . . .

BRUNCH

Brunch: the most important meal of the weekend! Nothing beats a great lazy-day brunch, best eaten at approximately 10:45 a.m. in PJs with a full pot of really good coffee or perfectly prepared tea. If you're fortunate enough to have the whole day to relax, then brunch cocktails are a must!

Some of the best brunches I've enjoyed have been on our travels—King's Highway diner at the Ace Hotel in Palm Springs, the Breslin at the Ace Hotel in New York and Little Goat Diner in Chicago making up my top three. Each one had the brunch trifecta down to a tee: deliciously decadent comfort food, a cozy, laid-back atmosphere and impeccable yet casual service.

Brunch is also the perfect time to pull out all your delicious preserve creations!

**A note on preserve pairings: Three perfect preserves that go particularly well with each dish appear at the bottom of each recipe in this part of the book, but I hope you'll improvise at will! The recipes will work equally well with whatever similar fruit jam or preserve you have on hand.

BRUNCH

{SERVES FOUR}

I know, I know . . . a "recipe" for toast? It's more of a suggested amalgamation of ingredients—totally open for interpretation—and when you find that perfect balance of acidity, saltiness and creaminess, it's truly a worthwhile endeavor.

For each recipe, use the best bread you can find—a "well-hydrated" *pain de campagne* if possible, the kind that sticks to your teeth a wee bit.

TOAST TRIO

Avocado Toast

2 perfectly ripe avocados
Juice from 1 lemon
1 tsp olive oil
Pinch of salt
Pinch of Aleppo or Espelette pepper
1 fresh cayenne chile pepper, seeds and
pith removed and sliced fine
Preserves to taste (suggestions below)

1. Simply mash, drizzle, sprinkle, spread
   on toast and top off with a spoonful
   of your favorite preserve.

THREE PERFECT PRESERVES:
Chile Pepper, 82
Beet with Oranges & Pink Peppercorn, 81
Pineapple with Mint & Chile, 106

Spiced Walnut Butter Toast

2 lb walnut pieces, toasted at 350°F
for 10 to 15 minutes
2 Tbsp sugar
1 tsp salt
¼ tsp ground ginger
¼ tsp ground white pepper
¼ cup olive oil
(plus a bit more if necessary)
Preserves to taste (suggestions below)

1. Process all ingredients except
   preserves in a food processor. You
   may need to add a little more oil to
   reach spreadable consistency.
2. Spread on toast, add your favorite
   preserve and enjoy! (The walnut
   butter will keep in the fridge for
   up to 3 months.)

THREE PERFECT PRESERVES:
Damson Plum & Sweet Vermouth, 51
Raspberry with Merlot & Peppercorn, 43
Plain Ol' Wild Blackberry, 61

Ricotta Toast

3 cups whole organic milk
1 cup heavy cream
1 tsp salt
3 Tbsp fresh lemon juice
Preserves to taste (suggestions below)

1. Line a sieve with two layers of cheesecloth and place over a large bowl.
2. Heat milk, cream and salt just to a boil, about 180°F to 200°F, stirring often with a heatproof spatula to prevent scorching and keeping a close eye on it so it doesn't boil over.
3. Remove from heat and gently stir in lemon juice. Let sit undisturbed for 5 minutes.
4. Gently ladle into the prepared cheesecloth-lined sieve. Drain until it reaches the desired consistency; 30 to 40 minutes is perfect for a softish warm curd.
5. Pile ricotta onto toast. Sprinkle with coarse pepper and top with a dollop of preserves.

NOTE: Yields about 1¹/₂ cups and keeps in the fridge for up to 4 days.

✥

THREE PERFECT PRESERVES:
Blood Orange with Coconut & Lillet, 101
Rhubarb with Ginger & Orange Zest, 31
Fig with Honey & Star Anise, 62

{ S E R V E S   F O U R }

This hearty breakfast will keep you going for the morning and most of the afternoon! It's stick-to-your-ribs-type food, perfect for cold mornings—and next-day leftovers are even better. Any dried fruit and nut combination works well, so use whatever you have in the pantry. Keep it simple! (Yes, I realize bruléeing breakfast sounds a little over the top. It's not totally necessary, but the lovely added crunch, not to mention the show, takes this oatmeal to another level.)

BRULÉED STEEL-CUT OATMEAL

1 Tbsp unsalted butter

1 cup steel-cut oats

1 tsp salt (flaked vanilla salt would be lovely)

½ tsp ground cardamom

½ tsp ground cinnamon

2 cups boiling water

2 cups almond milk

¼ cup dried apricots, chopped

¼ cup dates, chopped

¼ cup unsweetened shredded coconut

¼ cup toasted and chopped hazelnuts

¼ cup chopped pear

¼ cup fresh raspberries

For each serving . . .

1 Tbsp preserves (suggestions below)

1 Tbsp granulated sugar to brulée

1. Melt butter in a cast-iron skillet on medium-high heat. Add oats, salt and spices and cook until slightly toasted, 3 to 4 minutes, stirring often.

2. Add boiling water and simmer until oats begin to soften, approximately 15 minutes.

3. Add almond milk and dried fruits and continue to simmer until most of the liquid is gone.

4. Add coconut, nuts and fresh fruit; continue cooking until warmed through, about 3 to 5 more minutes.

5. To serve, ladle oatmeal into bowls, stir in preserves and sprinkle sugar in an even layer over top. Torch top until sugar caramelizes. If you don't have a kitchen torch, place under broiler on high, keeping a VERY close eye so you don't burn the top.

THREE PERFECT PRESERVES:

Banana with Passion Fruit & Rum, 98 | *Persimmon with Cinnamon & Pecans, 109*

Blood Orange with Coconut & Lillet, 101

{ SERVES FOUR }

There's a great café in Whistler, British Columbia, that does the best brunch. Their stuffed French toast is about 4 inches thick and filled with ham and cheese. I've never seen anyone finish a full order, but it is delicious. This riff on that dish is a quarter of the size, but still over the top, crazy rich and full of drippy, gooey, sweet, cheesy goodness. I highly recommend a good long walk (or nap) after you've wiped the cheese off your chin.

BRIE & PRESERVE–STUFFED FRENCH TOAST

1 unsliced loaf of brioche
1 small round of Brie (6 to 8 oz),
    cut into ¼-inch-thick slices
½ cup preserves (suggestions below)
2 Tbsp unsalted butter
Maple syrup to serve

Custard

4 eggs
½ cup whole milk
½ cup heavy cream
Pinch fresh-grated nutmeg
¼ cup sugar
Pinch of salt

1. Preheat oven to 350°F and line two baking sheets with parchment paper.
2. Slice bread into 1-inch slices and cut a 4-inch slit along the top crust of each slice to form a pocket.
3. Place a slice of Brie and a good smear of preserves into each piece of bread.
4. Whisk custard ingredients together. Dip both sides of filled bread slices into custard, place on a parchment-lined baking sheet and let sit for 3 to 5 minutes to fully absorb the custard.
5. Heat a large nonstick pan over medium-high heat. Add a pat of butter to the hot pan and fry each slice of custard-soaked bread until golden on both sides. Place slices on the second baking sheet and bake for 10 to 15 minutes until puffed and golden.
6. Serve with warm maple syrup and extra preserves.

❧

THREE PERFECT PRESERVES:
Strawberry with Pistachio & Vanilla, 32 | *Grilled Peach with Blackberry & Candied Ginger, 52*
Heritage Apple with Bacon & Scotch, 73

Strawberry with Pistachio & Vanilla, recipe page 32

Thought I'd share this quick vinaigrette recipe. It's our house go-to. I use almost any preserve that has either a herb or spice—Beet with Oranges & Pink Peppercorn (page 81), Fig with Honey & Star Anise (page 62) or the Blueberry & French Thyme (page 44) all work beautifully. I hope you enjoy!

THE PRESERVATORY VINAIGRETTE

1 Tbsp grainy Dijon
3 Tbsp preserves (suggestions above)
1 shallot, peeled and finely chopped
⅓ cup balsamic vinegar
1 cup olive oil
Salt to taste
Pink peppercorns to taste

1. Whisk together Dijon and preserves to combine. Add shallot, balsamic vinegar, then whisk in olive oil in a steady stream. Season with salt and pink peppercorns to taste. Keeps refrigerated up to 10 days.

{SERVES FOUR}

Truly, take any combination of grain, veg, spice, egg, cheese and herb and you've got a delicious and nutritious start to the day, perfect for hardworking farmers and busy families alike.

BREKKIE BOWL

4 slices prosciutto,
   pan-fried until crisp
4 perfectly poached
   eggs
¼ cup preserves
   (suggestions below)
¼ cup chopped cilantro
4 radishes, thinly sliced
1 chile pepper,
   seeds removed
   and finely chopped
¼ cup crumbled feta
   cheese
Pinch of flaked sea salt

Farro
1 cup farro
3 cups water
½ tsp curry powder
Pinch of salt
2 tsp lemon juice
2 tsp olive oil

Quinoa
1 cup quinoa
2 cups almond milk
1 cup water
½ tsp ground
   cardamom
Pinch of salt

Creamy Avocado Dressing
2 perfectly ripe
   avocados
¼ cup Greek yogurt
¼ cup fresh lemon
   juice
¼ cup olive oil
½ tsp Dijon
1 tsp Sriracha or
   other hot sauce
1 tsp salt

1. Rinse farro in cold water, then combine with water, curry powder and salt in a small saucepan. Bring to a boil over medium-high heat, reduce heat, cover pot and simmer until liquid is absorbed and farro is tender, about 20 to 30 minutes. Remove from heat and dress grains with lemon juice, olive oil and another pinch of salt if needed.

2. Rinse quinoa in cold water, then combine with the rest of the quinoa ingredients in a small saucepan. Bring to a boil over medium-high heat, reduce heat, cover pot and simmer until quinoa is tender, about 15 minutes.

3. For the avocado dressing, process all ingredients in a food processor or blender until smooth.

4. To assemble, divide grains into bowls—farro on one side, quinoa on the other. Crumble crispy prosciutto over top or place full slices into grains. Place egg onto grains, follow with a good dollop of avocado dressing and a spoonful of preserves, and garnish with remaining ingredients.

THREE PERFECT PRESERVES:

Olive with Orange & Lemon, 93 | *Heirloom Tomato & Chile, 66* | *Beet with Oranges & Pink Peppercorn, 81*

{MAKES APPROXIMATELY 2 DOZEN 2-INCH ROUND SCONES}

Always searching for the perfect scone, my mum got her hands on this recipe years ago. We've tweaked it a teeny bit, but if it ain't broke . . . The real secret is keeping everything cold and not overworking the dough. It might seem like way too much baking powder, but it's not. The unbaked scones freeze beautifully.

MUM'S BUTTERMILK SCONES

4½ cups all-purpose flour
1 cup sugar
⅓ cup baking powder
1 cup cold unsalted butter
4 eggs
Seeds from one vanilla bean

1 cup buttermilk
1 egg whisked with 1 tsp water for
  egg wash
2 Tbsp medium-coarse white sugar
Preserves (suggestions below) and
  clotted cream for serving

1. Preheat oven to 375°F and line a baking sheet with parchment paper.
2. In a large mixing bowl, whisk dry ingredients together. Cut in cold butter with a pastry cutter or grate in with a large-hole grater (much quicker and easier). Rub the butter and flour mixture gently with your fingers to combine until butter pieces are about ¼ inch in size.
3. In a separate bowl, whisk together 4 eggs, vanilla seeds and buttermilk.
4. Make a well in the dry ingredients and pour in the egg mixture. Stir just until combined and knead together gently, about 3 to 4 turns.
5. Roll out on a well-floured surface to about ½-inch thick, and cut out scones to desired shape and size. Place on parchment-lined baking sheet about 1 inch apart, brush with egg wash and sprinkle with sugar. Bake just until beginning to turn golden, about 10 to 12 minutes or longer if you are making larger scones.
6. Serve with preserves and clotted cream (if you can find it), or simply whip heavy cream for a traditional Scottish tea.

THREE PERFECT PRESERVES:
Rhubarb & Vanilla, 29 | *Strawberry & Roses, 34* | *Pear & Vanilla Bean, 76*

{SERVES FOUR}

Crepes are such a great vehicle for preserves. You can go all sweet like we did here, or add cheese and prosciutto for a savory take. This crepe batter keeps well, covered, for up to 3 days in the fridge.

BEST CREPES EVER!

2 cups all-purpose flour

¼ cup sugar

1 tsp salt

2 Tbsp olive oil

3 eggs

Zest of 1 medium orange

2 cups whole milk

¼ cup unsalted butter, melted

Good splash of liqueur, such as brandy, Grand Marnier or kirsch

Butter for cooking crepes

Preserves (suggestions below) and whipped cream for serving

1. Whisk dry ingredients together.
2. Combine oil and eggs in a separate bowl and whisk to combine.
3. Add orange zest to milk and add into egg mixture.
4. Whisk wet ingredients into dry, then add the melted butter and whisk until smooth. Stir in liqueur.
5. Refrigerate overnight for best results; take out of fridge 30 minutes before using.
6. Heat crepe pan or 8-inch non-stick frying pan and brush with a small amount of butter. Pour just enough batter to cover the pan so your crepes are nice and thin. Cook crepes evenly on both sides until nice and brown. Add more butter to the pan after every 4 to 5 crepes.
7. Serve with a variety of preserves or other toppings—and, of course, a side of whipped cream is never a bad idea!

❧

THREE PERFECT PRESERVES:

Seville Orange with Cardamom & Brandy, 110 | *Raspberry with Chocolate & Brandy, 43*
Banana with Passion Fruit & Rum, 98

{SERVES FOUR}

Part popover, part crepe, a Dutch baby is typically served sweet with sugar and a squeeze of lemon, which is lovely. However, this savory version, inspired by a delicious brunch in Brooklyn, is the cat's pajamas, as they say. Feel free to change the herb and cheese combinations as desired.

SAVORY DUTCH BABY

¾ cup all-purpose flour

¼ cup sugar

¼ tsp salt

3 eggs

¾ cup whole milk

2 Tbsp unsalted butter

2 Tbsp chopped fresh tarragon

4 slices prosciutto

¼ cup grated Gruyère

Preserves to taste (suggestions below)

1. Preheat oven to 425°F.
2. In a medium bowl, combine dry ingredients and whisk. Add eggs and milk and whisk well into a smooth, thin batter.
3. Assemble all other ingredients to have close at hand.
4. Heat an 8-inch cast-iron skillet on high heat. Add butter to skillet. When butter melts and is bubbling hot, pour in batter, turn off heat, sprinkle with tarragon, lay prosciutto over top and sprinkle Gruyère evenly over all. Put straight into the hot oven. Don't peek for at least 15 minutes. Bake until golden and puffed, 15 to 18 minutes.
5. Serve hot, the faster the better—this baby falls quickly—with a dollop of preserves.

❧

THREE PERFECT PRESERVES:

Pear & Vanilla Bean, 76 | *Heirloom Tomato & Chile, 66* | *Apricot with Tarragon & Riesling, 48*

{SERVES FOUR}

Mmm, cheesy grits . . . I was *so* excited to shoot this recipe, just to have the excuse to keep "testing" it. It's really simple, so satisfying and a wee bit decadent. If you ever get to San Francisco, go to the Ferry Building and order the cheesy grits at Cowgirl Creamery. This recipe is a toss-up between those and the grits with fire-roasted chiles at King's Highway diner in Palm Springs—both some of the best grits I've ever had.

CHEESY GRITS

1 cup whole milk
1 cup water
Pinch of salt
½ cup coarse-ground cornmeal
2 Tbsp unsalted butter
½ cup grated aged cheddar
¼ cup grated Parmesan

Assembly

4 slices pancetta, cooked crisp and chopped
1 poblano pepper, charred on the grill, stem and
seeds removed, and chopped
¼ cup preserves (suggestions below)
4 soft-poached eggs

1.   Bring milk, water and salt to a boil in a medium saucepan.
2.   Add cornmeal in a slow, steady stream, whisking constantly. Simmer, uncovered, until thickened, about 20 minutes, stirring every 5 minutes.
3.   Remove from heat and stir in butter and cheeses.
4.   Serve hot, garnishing each serving with pancetta, chopped peppers, preserves and a poached egg.

THREE PERFECT PRESERVES:
Heirloom Tomato & Chile, 66 | Heritage Apple with Bacon & Scotch, 73
Moroccan-Spiced Sour Cherry, 38

{ SERVES FOUR TO SIX }

One of my favorite desserts turned into a brunch treat, these are seriously awesome! The tropical twist of adding the Piña Colada preserves proved to be the ultimate pairing, but many other preserves would work with this recipe. These were gobbled up during the photo shoot, nary a crumb left behind!

CARROT CAKE WAFFLES

2 cups all-purpose flour
2 tsp baking powder
½ tsp salt
¼ cup sugar
2 tsp ground cinnamon
½ whole nutmeg, grated
4 eggs, separated
½ cup unsalted butter, melted

1 cup whole milk
1 cup grated carrots
½ cup preserves (suggestions below)
¼ cup chopped walnuts
¼ cup raisins
¼ cup unsweetened shredded coconut
Maple syrup and whipped cream
    for serving

1. Combine dry ingredients in a large mixing bowl.
2. In a separate bowl, whisk egg whites until stiff peaks form. Set aside.
3. In yet another bowl, whisk together egg yolks, butter and milk. Blend well into dry mixture. Fold in grated carrots, preserves, walnuts, raisins and coconut. Lastly, fold in egg whites.
4. Pour batter into a waffle maker and cook as per the manufacturer's instructions.
5. Serve with warm maple syrup, whipped cream and extra preserves.

❧

THREE PERFECT PRESERVES:

Persimmon with Cinnamon & Pecans, 109 | *Seville Orange with Cardamom & Brandy, 110* | *Piña Colada, 106*

{ SERVES FOUR TO SIX }

These delicious "jamcakes" have a sweet surprise interior and crunchy sweet exterior. Kids love 'em almost as much as adults do! The addition of ricotta balances out the sweetness and takes away some of the guilt. Serve with demerara and pepper bacon knots (see note) for an extra-special Sunday morning and to add that guilt right back in!

NOTE: To make bacon knots—just like they sound—use a regular sliced bacon as opposed to thick. Tie bacon strips in a loose knot and sprinkle with demerara sugar and black pepper. Bake on a parchment-lined baking sheet at 375°F until caramelized, about 15 to 20 minutes.

NUTTY RICOTTA JAMCAKES

2 cups all-purpose flour

2 tsp baking powder

1 tsp baking soda

½ tsp salt

¼ tsp fresh-grated nutmeg

3 Tbsp sugar

2 eggs

1 cup ricotta (see Ricotta Toast, page 117, for homemade, or store-bought works just as well)

2 cups whole milk

¼ cup unsalted butter, melted

1 cup preserves (suggestions below)

1 cup chopped Easy Candied Pecans (recipe opposite)

Maple syrup for serving

1. Whisk together dry ingredients in large bowl to combine. In separate bowl, whisk together eggs, ricotta, milk and melted butter. Pour wet mixture into dry and whisk to combine into semi-smooth batter.
2. Heat skillet or frying pan and brush with butter. Drop about 2 tablespoons of batter onto the bubbling butter, add a teaspoon of jam in the middle of each round of batter, cover each with a teaspoon more batter and sprinkle with pecans. Brown jamcakes evenly on both sides.
3. Serve with warm maple syrup and extra preserves.

❧

THREE PERFECT PRESERVES:

Plain Ol' Wild Blackberry, 61 | Heritage Apple with Bacon & Scotch, 73
Raspberry with Chocolate & Brandy, 43

These are so great to have on hand!

EASY CANDIED PECANS

1 egg white
½ cup demerara sugar
1 tsp ground cinnamon
1 tsp salt
½ tsp fresh-grated nutmeg
½ tsp cayenne pepper
4 cups pecans

1. Preheat oven to 350°F.
2. Whisk together egg white, demerara sugar, cinnamon, salt, nutmeg and cayenne. Stir in pecans until well coated.
3. Pour onto parchment-lined baking sheet and bake 10 to 15 minutes, stirring every 5 minutes to ensure even browning, until dry and crispy.
4. Store in an airtight container for 2 to 3 weeks.

{SERVES ONE HUNGRY FARMER}

This is what happens when you are starving and have a weirdly stocked fridge—one weirdly delicious sandwich!

UNLIKELY REUBEN

Rye bread
Endive & Radicchio "Kimchi"
(page 231)
Pineapple with Mint & Chile preserve
(page 106)
Hot mustard
Corned beef
Thousand Island dressing
Swiss cheese
Butter for cooking sandwiches

1. Top half of the rye bread slices with the rest of the ingredients and cover with the remaining bread slices.
2. Butter the top and bottom of each sandwich and grill it in a hot skillet or frying pan to get the cheese nice and melty!
3. Enjoy!

Curried Hollandaise

2 egg yolks
1 Tbsp fresh lemon juice
1 tsp Dijon
1 tsp curry powder
½ cup unsalted butter, melted
Salt and pepper to taste

1. Using a double boiler over simmering water, whisk egg yolks, lemon juice, Dijon and curry powder. Whisk until thickened, but not scrambled!

2. Off heat, slowly add warm melted butter drop by drop, whisking continuously, about 3 to 5 minutes, until thick. If hollandaise begins to split, whisk in a few drops of ice-cold water until it comes back together.

3. Season with salt and pepper to taste. Keep warm over double boiler off heat.

{SERVES FOUR}

I love a good breakfast hash, and so does my husband, Patrick—and this skillet mixture is our new favorite! It's been taken to the next level with the addition of a curried hollandaise and, of course, a little bit o' jam! Don't be intimidated by the hollandaise; if it totally separates, simply whisk in some mayo and you'll be back to looking like a pro.

HEARTY SKILLET HASH

1 Tbsp olive oil
1 shallot, chopped
10 mushrooms, chopped
2 bell peppers, chopped
2 green onions, chopped
2 Tbsp chopped fresh tarragon
2 cups shredded pork belly (page 147)
   or duck rillettes (page 159)
2 sweet potatoes, peeled, chopped and
   roasted or pan-fried with olive oil
   and salt and pepper

Assembly

4 perfectly fried eggs
Preserves (suggestions below)
Curried Hollandaise (recipe opposite)
Flaked sea salt and freshly
   ground pepper

1. Heat a cast-iron skillet over medium-high heat. Add oil to the hot pan and sauté shallots and mushrooms until nicely browned. Add in bell peppers, green onions and tarragon and sauté until peppers are softened. Stir in shredded pork or duck and sweet potatoes; continue cooking until everything is nice and hot.

2. Serve hash piled on each plate, with a perfect egg balanced on top, a dollop of preserves and a velvety slick of hollandaise. Season with flaked sea salt and freshly ground pepper. Add a side of toast to sop up all the deliciousness.

THREE PERFECT PRESERVES:
Sweet Potato Pie, 85 | *Indian-Spiced Green Tomato, 89* | *Heirloom Tomato & Chile, 66*

APERITIVO

My favorite way to eat! I'm much happier with a bunch of little bits of deliciousness than one big meal. It means a little more work, but gives you the ability to let your creativity fly. Do-ahead recipes are a godsend and make having friends over for cocktails a breeze. Make it easy on yourself; the more you prepare in advance, the more you'll get to relax and enjoy yourself and your company! Many of these recipes can be prepped and thrown in the freezer for impromptu invites—usually the best kind!

Hors d'oeuvres, appetizers, starters—all are in the same family as aperitivo, but with a different upbringing. Aperitivo is this wonderful phenomenon in Italy—specifically, Milano. Similar to happy hour, yet so different. Depending on where you end up, you order a cocktail, albeit a very overpriced cocktail, and you get plate after plate of little lovely bites of deliciousness. After one of my favorite aperitivo in Milano, we were so completely stuffed we had to cancel our dinner reservations, and if you know my husband, Patrick, or me, that is a very rare occurrence. We don't miss many meals, especially when we're travelling; my FOMO game is very strong!

APERITIVO

NOTE: Easy Candied Pecans also make a great little bite (recipe page 137)

{MAKES APPROXIMATELY 12 TO 14 CROQUETTES}

One of my favorite restaurants—okay, perhaps my favorite—is in Paris, no surprise, and it boasts the longest lunch wait in St. Germain: Le Comptoir du Relais. The dish I love most is the brandade—a traditional salt cod/potato mash-up that they broil and serve in rustic ceramic dishes; the top is crunchy and the bottom is creamy deliciousness. This is my attempt to create more of that lovely crunch while keeping the luscious creaminess inside. Of course, the addition of preserves to finish it with a little sweetness is my own contribution. *Bon appétit*!

BRANDADE CROQUETTES

1 lb salt cod

¼ cup olive oil, warmed

½ cup whole milk, warmed

2 cups russet potatoes,
    peeled and cubed

¼ cup unsalted butter

¼ cup heavy cream

2 egg yolks

Salt and pepper to taste

½ tsp fresh-grated nutmeg

½ cup all-purpose flour

1 egg whisked with 1 tsp water for
    egg wash

½ cup panko bread crumbs

Vegetable oil for frying

1. Soak salt cod in water for 30 minutes. Remove to a small saucepan and cover cod with fresh water. Bring to a simmer and poach until falling apart (about 10 to 15 minutes). Strain cod and remove any remaining bones. With a wooden spoon, mash cod into a paste. Drizzle warm olive oil into cod and stir until fully incorporated. Stir in warm milk to finish cod mixture.

2. Meanwhile, boil potatoes in salted water about 15 to 20 minutes until tender. Drain, then strain and mash with butter, cream and egg yolks. Season to taste with salt, pepper and nutmeg. Combine mashed potato with mashed cod, blending well, then cool completely.

3. Place flour, egg wash, and panko on separate plates or in shallow containers.

4. Shape the cod/potato mash into logs or balls, about 2 inches in size. Dredge each in flour, dip in the egg wash and roll in the panko.

5. Fry a few at a time in oil heated to 350°F until golden and crisp. Remove with a slotted spoon and drain on paper towel. Keep warm in a low oven (250°F). Serve hot with preserves.

THREE PERFECT PRESERVES:

Beet with Oranges & Pink Peppercorn, 81 | *Blueberry & French Thyme, 44* | *Fig with Honey & Star Anise, 62*

Chef Robert Clark, arguably British Columbia's most notable seafood chef and a strong supporter of the sustainable seafood movement, served this deliciousness with our preserves at an event over 10 years ago— a total "aha" moment for me to have the preserves used in a savory application. He served this crispy pork belly with our Green Tomato & Garam Masala preserve. I loved it so much that I added it to my catering menus; but first I emailed him to ask for some of his trade secrets for cooking the pork. This was his reply:

The secret is cooking it at a very low temp, 190–200°F, for a very long time, like overnight, slow slow slow. Water, wine and a few aromatics and it should come out tasting great.

After it is cooked it will need to be pressed and cooled before you can cut it. Have fun—Rob.

This recipe takes time (three days) and it's a bit of work, but so worth it. What's more, you can freeze the extra pork belly to add to ramen, a breakfast skillet, or really anything that needs a little extra porky richness.

CRISPY PORK BELLY BITES

1 to 2 lb pork belly, rind scored

Dry Rub	Braising Liquid
1 tsp fennel seeds	2 cups water
1 tsp coriander seeds	2 cups wine or dry apple cider
1 tsp black peppercorns	5 bay leaves
4 whole star anise	6 whole star anise
½ tsp ground cinnamon	12 cardamom pods
⅛ tsp ground cloves	1 Tbsp fennel seeds
2 Tbsp coarse sea salt	1 medium onion, sliced
2 Tbsp demerara sugar	2 medium oranges, zest and juice

1. Grind dry rub ingredients with a mortar and pestle or in a spice grinder. Rub spices all over pork belly and wrap tightly with plastic wrap. Refrigerate overnight.
2. The next day, preheat oven to 200°F, remove plastic wrap from the pork and brush off as much of the rub as you easily can. Place pork fat side up in a roasting pan that's as close to the same size as the belly as possible.
3. Add all braising liquid ingredients to the pan and cover tightly with foil. Braise for about 10 to 12 hours until pork belly is falling-apart tender. When done, remove from oven and cool in braising liquid.
4. Remove cooled pork from pan and wrap tightly in plastic wrap. Place on a tray in the fridge with a heavy plate or pan on top to keep pressure on the pork. Refrigerate overnight to make pork easier to slice.
5. Remove from fridge and slice into ½-inch slabs and then into 1-inch pieces. In a dry cast-iron skillet, fry on both sides until crispy. Serve hot with a dollop of preserves.

THREE PERFECT PRESERVES:
Pineapple with Mint & Chile, 106 | *Indian-Spiced Green Tomato, 89* | *Moroccan-Spiced Sour Cherry, 38*

{SERVES TWO}

I wish I could remember where I tasted my first butter-grilled oysters—maybe Joël Robuchon Atelier? Yep, that's it! We sat at the bar and our server explained every detail of the menu, including how they made their lovely butter-poached oysters. These are so easy and delicious, you may need more than a dozen oysters. A Kir Preserve Royale (page 234) would be the perfect accompaniment.

BUTTER-BBQ'D OYSTERS

1 dozen oysters
6 tsp Compound Jam Butter
(a spicy combo is best;
see page 151)
2 slices bacon or pancetta, cooked crisp
and chopped fine
3 Tbsp freshly grated horseradish

1. Heat grill to medium-high and shuck oysters. Place ½ tsp compound butter in center of each oyster.
2. Place oysters on grill, close lid and count to 30. Lift lid and sprinkle oysters with crispy bacon bits. Carefully remove oysters from grill with tongs so you don't spill any of the yummy sauce that has been created.
3. Serve hot oysters with a pinch of freshly grated horseradish.

❧

THREE PERFECT PRESERVES FOR COMPOUND BUTTERS:
Heirloom Tomato & Chile, 66 | Spicy Sweet Charred Onion & Figs, 86
Indian-Spiced Green Tomato, 89

Compound Jam Butters

1 cup unsalted butter, softened

3 Tbsp preserves

(suggestions below)

1 Tbsp aromatic

(see suggested combinations below)

1 tsp flaked sea salt

1. Blend ingredients together in a food processor.
2. Form into a log, wrap in parchment and refrigerate
   2 hours before using. Butters will keep in the fridge for
   5 to 7 days or in the freezer for up to 3 months.

❧

SPICY COMBOS

Heirloom Tomato & Chile (page 66) with chile pepper flakes

Spicy Sweet Charred Onion & Figs (page 86) with fresh chile peppers

Indian-Spiced Green Tomato (page 89) with garam masala

HERBY COMBOS

Apricot with Tarragon & Riesling (page 48) with fresh tarragon

Olive with Orange & Lemon (page 93) with fresh thyme

Chile Pepper (page 82) with cilantro

SWEET COMBOS

Rhubarb with Ginger & Orange Zest (page 31) with orange zest

Raspberry with Chocolate & Brandy (page 43) with cocoa powder

Fig with Honey & Star Anise (page 62) with honeycomb

Crostini 101

Crostini—the perfect cocktail party food! Drizzle olive oil over thinly sliced baguette, season with salt, and toast at 350°F for 3 to 5 minutes. A few suggested combinations are below. Feel free to create your own, to match your pantry's inventory!

TOPPED WITH . . .

Apricot with Tarragon & Riesling (page 48), smoked trout, avocado, radishes, beets

Chestnut with Dates & Brandy (page 100), beef carpaccio, horseradish cream, orange segments

Fig with Honey & Star Anise (page 62), prosciutto, blue cheese, walnuts

Spicy Pickled Brussels Sprouts (page 229), crispy pancetta, Gorgonzola

Endive & Radicchio "Kimchi" (page 231), pork belly, avocado, scallions

Chile Pepper (page 82), shrimp, queso fresco, cilantro

Spicy Sweet Charred Onion & Figs (page 86), Boursin, quail egg, crispy onions

Spicy Sweet Charred Onion & Figs, recipe page 86

I served this at our first Feast of Fields, an annual event hosted by FarmFolk CityFolk, here at the farm to about 800 people—overwhelming, to say the least! These little grilled bites are a perfect make-ahead recipe and are great to serve at a lazy summer BBQ. Make the polenta the day before, then simply cut and grill right before cocktail hour begins. Perfect with a glass of bubbly!

GRILLED POLENTA & BLUE CHEESE

4½ cups water
1 tsp salt
1 cup coarse-ground cornmeal
¼ cup chopped fresh herbs
(tarragon, chive or parsley)
1 tsp black pepper
¼ cup crumbled blue cheese
Olive oil for grilling polenta
Preserves to taste (suggestions below)

1. Line a baking sheet with parchment.
2. Bring water and salt to a boil. Add cornmeal while whisking, and continue stirring for about 5 to 10 minutes until thick. Stir in herbs and pepper.
3. Pour onto parchment-lined baking sheet and sprinkle blue cheese evenly over top while still warm. Let cool overnight.
4. Cut into small rounds or squares, brush bottoms with olive oil and grill, cheese side up, over medium heat, just to warm through. Serve hot with preserves.

❧

THREE PERFECT PRESERVES:
Spicy Sweet Charred Onion & Figs, 86 | Heirloom Tomato & Chile, 66
Sweet Corn with Espelette & Chardonnay, 65

{ MAKES ABOUT 2 DOZEN }

Warning: these little Indian-spiced bites pack a punch and, served with a wee bit of sweet preserve, are highly addictive! Inspired by many meals at Vij's Restaurant in Vancouver and one very memorable meal with Meeru and Vikram in their home, this became a catering menu staple of mine for many events. They are so great to have on hand in the freezer—an easy do-ahead that every party planner can appreciate!

INDIAN-SPICED LAMB BALLS

1 lb ground lamb

1 lb ground pork

2 eggs, lightly whisked

¼ cup preserves (suggestions below)

1 cup bread crumbs

2 jalapeños, finely chopped

3 cloves garlic, minced

1 cup chopped cilantro

2 Tbsp garam masala

1 Tbsp ground ginger

2 tsp salt

1 tsp cayenne pepper

1 Tbsp olive oil, for frying

1. Preheat oven to 350°F.
2. Combine and gently mix all ingredients, except for the olive oil, well to fully blend flavors. Form into small, one-bite round balls.
3. Heat olive oil in a frying pan and sear lamb balls until evenly browned. Transfer to a baking dish or baking sheet and finish in the oven for 10 to 15 minutes or until cooked through. Serve hot with preserves.

THREE PERFECT PRESERVES:

Indian-Spiced Green Tomato, 89 | Mulled Wine Jelly, 102 | Chile Pepper, 82

Little-known fact: according to *Larousse Gastronomique*, Honoré de Balzac called rillettes "brown jam" in his book *Le Lys dans la vallée* and so this recipe almost belongs in Part I of this book. You can find confit duck legs in most specialty grocers or at your local butcher. They are usually covered in a lovely layer of fat . . . don't throw it away—use it for your rillettes and store any leftover fat in the freezer for future duck-fat-fried potato cravings!

{ SERVES FOUR TO SIX }

DUCK RILLETTES WITH CHIVE CAKES

Duck Rillettes

6 confit duck legs (see note opposite)
¼ to ½ cup duck fat removed from legs,
melted, divided
½ cup rice wine vinegar
2 Tbsp preserves (suggestions below)
1 shallot, minced
1 chile pepper, seeded and minced
1 tsp grated fresh ginger
Zest and juice of 1 small orange
1 Tbsp mirin
Salt (if needed)

1. Remove skin from duck legs and
   discard. Remove meat and place
   in the bowl of a standup mixer
   fitted with the paddle attachment
   or mash with a wooden spoon.
   Mix until meat is well shredded but
   not mushy.
2. Add ¼ cup melted duck fat and
   remaining ingredients; mix until
   well combined.
3. Place mixture in small ramekins
   or jam jars and top with extra
   melted fat to help preserve. Keep
   refrigerated for up to one week.

Chive Cakes

1 ½ cups all-purpose flour
¾ cup warm water
2 tsp sesame oil
1 tsp salt
2 Tbsp chopped chives
Olive oil for frying

1. Mix flour and water into a dough
   and knead until smooth. Leave to
   rise in oiled bowl for 30 minutes.
2. Divide dough and form into small
   1-inch balls. Roll each ball out into
   a round and lay the rounds on a
   parchment-lined baking sheet.
3. Brush half the rounds with sesame
   oil and sprinkle with salt and chives.
   Cover with the other rounds, press
   the edges to seal and roll out thin.
4. Fry chive cakes in very hot, but not
   smoking olive oil and serve topped
   with Duck Rillettes and preserves.

*NOTE: In a pinch (or if time-crunched),
you can use store-bought naan bread or
crepes instead of the chive cakes.*

❧

THREE PERFECT **PRESERVES:**
*Kumquat with Vanilla & Vodka, 97 | Rhubarb with **Ginger** & Orange Zest, 31
Rainier Cherry & Kirsch, 41*

{ONE 9-INCH SQUARE TART}

This is very loosely based on the best *pissaladière* I've ever had, from a tiny *traiteur* in Lourmarin. It was a crazy drive to get there, but well worth the cliff-hanging roads; Le Moulin de Lourmarin is a must-stop if you're ever in this region of France. Their version was on a "simple" piece of toast—one of the best pieces of toast I have ever eaten!

OLIVE & CARAMELIZED ONION TART

1 sheet or 8 oz frozen puff pastry, thawed

1 egg whisked with 1 tsp water for egg wash

2 Tbsp olive oil

1 medium onion, diced

1 tsp salt

2 cloves garlic, minced

1 tsp fresh thyme leaves

3 Tbsp heavy cream

3 Tbsp fresh goat cheese

1 Tbsp capers, drained and chopped

1 Tbsp lemon or orange zest

Freshly ground black pepper to taste

1 cup olives (Kalamata or other favorite), pitted and roughly chopped

½ cup preserves (suggestions below)

1. On a floured surface, roll out pastry into a 9½-inch square. Trim off ½-inch strips from each side. Brush egg wash around the edges of the rectangle and attach the cut-off strips to the edges, trimming excess as needed, to create a raised border.

2. Place pastry on a parchment-lined baking sheet and prick all over the middle of the rectangle with a fork. This will prevent your dough from puffing up in the middle. Refrigerate the dough while you're preparing the filling.

3. Preheat oven to 400°F.

4. For the filling, heat a sauté pan over medium-high heat. Add olive oil, then add the onions, salt, garlic and thyme. Sauté for 5 to 7 minutes, stirring occasionally, until caramelized and soft. Set aside to cool.

5. Stir cream, goat cheese, capers, zest and pepper into the cooled onion mixture and spread over the prepared pastry shell. Cover liberally with olives and dollops of preserves.

6. Brush edges with remaining egg wash and bake for 20 to 30 minutes or until pastry is golden.

THREE PERFECT PRESERVES:
Beet with Oranges & Pink Peppercorn, 81 | *Olive with Orange & Lemon, 93*
Spicy Sweet Charred Onion & Figs, 86

{ SERVES FOUR TO SIX }

Not all recipes have to be difficult! In fact, the easier the better in the summer, when the farm's at its craziest, when we're yelling at each other, "Hurry up!! Harvest the cherries before the damn crows figure out they're ready . . . again!" These are perfect at those hectic times, 'cause nothing beats a feast of chicken wings!

NOTE: These are also great baked at 375°F for 45 to 50 minutes. Be sure to glaze with preserves before baking.

GLAZED CHICKEN DRUMMETTES

2 lb chicken drummettes (organic or free range is best)
Kosher salt and freshly ground pepper to taste
1 cup preserves (suggestions below)

1. Season chicken with salt and pepper.
2. Grill over medium heat, turning often. Keep an eye on these; they're notorious for flare-ups! When cooked through, brush with preserves. Be generous and continue cooking just until the glaze nicely caramelizes.
3. Serve with extra preserves on the side for dipping.

❧

THREE PERFECT PRESERVES:
Mulled Wine Jelly, 102 | Chile Pepper, 82 | Smoked Lime Margarita, 105

DINNER

On the farm we typically make dinner late, and I usually do something quick and easy. There's always a hungry crowd and usually a tired cook, so simple and delicious is my go-to plan. We also do a few big farm-table meals during the year, and many of these dishes are perfect for larger groups; simply scale up accordingly.

Of course, inevitably and not surprisingly, preserves end up in many of our meals. They truly are versatile and are such a great way to add intense flavor and a little wow factor to dishes, especially ones you're doing on the fly! The fact that I have a dedicated shelf in my fridge for preserves may factor in slightly; we just call this section of the fridge the research and development department!

One of the best that came out of that R&D is the pizzam. Pizza + jam = Pizzam. A few years ago at Feast of Fields, an event held annually in Vancouver that brings together chefs, farmers, winemakers and brewers, my friend Mary Mackay from Terra Breads (the best bakery in the city) and I collaborated on an idea. Mary was making pizzas in her awesome "husband-built" pizza oven, and I was making PB&J sandwiches (actually brioche with Spiced Walnut Butter, page 116, and Plum with Vanilla & Star Anise preserve, page 58). We ended up combining the two to make some PB&J pizzams; the rest, as they say, is history!

DINNER

{ S E R V E S F O U R }

This is our go-to meal in the summer, when we're run off our feet and want a quick, delicious, guilt-free dinner.

N O T E : It's nice to use fresh fruit that mirrors the preserves you're using—fresh pineapple with the Pineapple with Mint & Chile preserves, for example.

GRILLED FLANK STEAK SALAD

One whole flank steak—about 2 lb

Marinade

½ cup soy sauce

½ cup preserves (suggestions below)

¼ cup rice wine vinegar

2 Tbsp sesame oil

1 tsp sambal oelek

2 cloves garlic, minced

2 tsp grated fresh ginger

1 bunch cilantro, stems only
  (reserve leaves for salad)

Zest and juice of 2 limes

Salad

2 bell peppers, quartered and seeded

2 sweet onions, cut into rounds

4 cups mixed greens, such as spinach,
  baby kale and watercress

1 cup chopped fresh fruit (see note)

2 to 3 Tbsp olive oil

¼ cup reserved marinade

Salt to taste

Reserved cilantro leaves,
  chopped, for garnish

½ cup chopped mint for garnish

1. For the marinade, whisk all ingredients in a medium bowl. Reserve ¼ cup for the salad dressing and place the remaining marinade in a large ziplock bag. Place flank steak in the bag and refrigerate for at least 1 hour and up to 12 hours.

2. When ready to prepare the meal, let the meat come to room temperature for about 30 minutes.

3. Preheat grill to medium-high heat. Grill peppers and onions; set aside. Grill flank steak to medium-rare, about 6 to 7 minutes per side. Let meat rest for about 15 minutes, then slice steak across the grain into thin slices.

4. Toss salad greens and chopped fruit together, dress with olive oil and reserved marinade and season with salt to taste. Serve greens with grilled veggies and sliced flank steak layered over top. Garnish with cilantro and mint.

THREE PERFECT PRESERVES:

Tomatillo & Chile, 90 | Chile Pepper, 82 | Pineapple with Mint & Chile, 106

{SERVES FOUR}

Sometimes only a big batch of Mama Ribs will do. These started out as Grandma Ribs—my grandma Gracie made them famous in our family, though I'm not sure where she got the original recipe from. My mum took over, and because the kids call her Mama . . . well, you get the idea. Life permitting, we have dinner together every Sunday, and more often than not, Mama Ribs are on the menu. I've changed the recipe only a bit, and I hope Grandma Gracie approves of the . . . ahem . . . enhancements. Serve with creamy mashed potatoes and roast veggies.

MAMA RIBS

2 racks baby back pork ribs, silver skin removed
Salt and pepper

Sauce

1 cup preserves (suggestions below)

1 cup water

½ cup ketchup

½ cup white wine vinegar

1 Tbsp Worcestershire sauce

1 tsp salt

½ tsp celery salt

4 dashes Tabasco (if you're using Chile Pepper as the preserve, you can skip this!)

1. In a small saucepan, whisk together all sauce ingredients, then bring to a simmer over medium-high heat, stirring constantly. Reduce heat to low and simmer for 5 minutes. Turn off heat and keep sauce warm.
2. Preheat oven to 425°F. Season ribs with salt and pepper. Roast on parchment-lined baking sheets until brown, about 5 to 7 minutes per side. Remove from oven and reduce temperature to 325°F. Slice racks into 2- to 3-rib portion sizes.
3. Place browned ribs into a deep roasting pan, pour sauce over, cover with foil and bake at 325°F for 2 hours until the ribs are falling-off-the-bone tender.

❧

THREE PERFECT PRESERVES:
Spicy Sweet Charred Onion & Figs, 86 | *Heirloom Tomato & Chile, 66* | *Chile Pepper, 82*

{SERVES FOUR}

We are so fortunate to live where we do, and I count wild salmon as one of the many benefits of coastal living. Thankfully I have a few fishermen in my family who keep our freezers well stocked, and in the summer there is nothing better than a fresh-off-the-grill fillet of sockeye salmon. This simple recipe is great for family BBQs. Serve with a warm potato salad dressed in red wine vinegar, grainy Dijon and olive oil along with a side of steamed green beans to round out the meal.

GRILLED WILD SALMON

1 side wild sockeye (if you can find it) salmon fillet, skin on, pin bones removed
½ cup preserves (suggestions below)
½ tsp salt

Marinade
1 Tbsp soy sauce or fresh lemon juice
1 Tbsp olive oil
1 clove garlic, minced
1 tsp grated fresh ginger

1. Heat grill to medium-high.
2. Whisk marinade ingredients in a small bowl. Place salmon on foil, skin side down, and pour marinade evenly over top. Let salmon sit in marinade for no more than 10 minutes, or it will cook without you.

3. Smear preserves on flesh side from tip to tail and place salmon on grill. Salmon is perfectly cooked when the fat begins to turn white at the tail end. Remove from heat so as not to overcook.

NOTE: If you're pressed for time or have run out of steam at dinnertime, as I often do, simply season salmon with salt in place of marinade and smear with preserves.

⤳

THREE PERFECT PRESERVES:
*Blueberry & French Thyme, 44 | Indian-Spiced Green Tomato, 89
Pineapple with Mint & Chile, 106*

Okay, so the recipe name is not super creative, but honestly, I could not think of a better word for this pork dish. Pork loves fruit, and this pan sauce, with the addition of preserves, is, well, delicious. Serve with a simple quinoa salad and freshly baked bread for mopping up the lovely sauce!

DELICIOUS PORK TENDERLOIN

1 or 2 pork tenderloin, about 1½ lb total

Pan Sauce

1 Tbsp olive oil
1 medium onion, sliced
1 clove garlic, minced
Pinch of salt
¼ cup brandy
1 Tbsp Dijon
½ cup preserves (suggestions below)
Zest and juice of 1 medium orange

Spice Rub

1 tsp peppercorns
1 tsp coriander seeds
1 tsp fennel seeds
1 tsp coarse salt
1 tsp demerara or brown sugar

1. Grind all rub ingredients in a spice grinder or using a mortar and pestle and pour into a ziplock bag large enough to hold tenderloin. Place tenderloin in the bag and give it a good shake to mash the spices all around the meat. Refrigerate for at least 30 minutes or up to 2 hours.
2. Preheat oven to 375°F and let pork come to room temperature for about 15 minutes.
3. Heat a cast-iron pan over medium-high heat. Add olive oil and sear all sides of the tenderloin about 2 minutes per side. Remove from the pan and keep warm.
4. Sauté onion and garlic with a pinch of salt for 5 to 7 minutes, until nicely caramelized. Carefully deglaze the pan with brandy, then stir in Dijon, preserves and orange zest and juice. Simmer sauce for 3 to 5 minutes, then snuggle pork back into the pan and place in the oven until the internal temperature of the pork comes to 140°F to 145°F, approximately 15 to 20 minutes.
5. Rest pork for 10 minutes, then slice and serve with pan sauce.

THREE PERFECT PRESERVES:
Moroccan-Spiced Sour Cherry, 38 | *Seville Orange with Cardamom & Brandy, 110*
Chestnut with Dates & Brandy, 100

Such a comfort food curry is. I can be a little heavy-handed when using spices, so the addition of coconut milk always helps balance this dish if I go a little crazy. This simple dish is also perfect for yummy leftovers (that is NOT an oxymoron!). I used chicken thighs, but you could cut up and use a whole fryer chicken for this recipe. Serve with aromatic basmati rice.

COCONUT CURRY BRAISED CHICKEN

6 to 8 bone-in, skinless chicken thighs
Salt and pepper for seasoning
1 Tbsp olive oil
1 tsp unsalted butter
1 medium onion, chopped
1 clove garlic, minced
1 Tbsp grated fresh ginger
1 Tbsp Madras curry powder
4 medium carrots, peeled and chopped

1 bunch broccolini stems, chopped and florets separated
1 red bell pepper, chopped
¼ cup white wine
1 cup light coconut milk
1 cup preserves (suggestions below)
1 cup sweet pea pods, trimmed
½ cup chopped cilantro

1. Season chicken thighs with salt and pepper.
2. Heat oil and butter in a large sauté pan over medium-high heat. Brown thighs well on both sides. Try not to crowd the pan; you may have to do it in a couple of batches. Remove chicken from pan and reserve.
3. In the same pan, sauté onion, garlic and ginger until soft, then add curry powder and sauté on medium-high heat another 2 to 3 minutes. Deglaze with wine and reduce for 3 minutes. Add carrots, broccolini stems and peppers to the pan and sauté 2 to 3 minutes.
4. Stir in coconut milk and preserves and add chicken thighs back in. Bring to a slow simmer and braise uncovered for 30 minutes, until chicken is tender. Add pea pods and broccolini florets and cook an additional 2 to 3 minutes.
5. Spoon over hot rice and garnish with chopped cilantro.

THREE PERFECT PRESERVES:
Piña Colada, 106 | Tomatillo & Chile, 90 | Indian-Spiced Green Tomato, 89

{SERVES SIX TO EIGHT}

The Moroccan-Spiced Sour Cherry preserve was the instigator of this creation—I had leftover spices, and my family loves roast lamb. This one is perfect for cold farm nights after long days of working outside in the rain crushing grapes or picking the last of a seemingly zillion pounds of apples in the fall. The couscous on its own is a great side with any roast meat.

ROAST LAMB & MOROCCAN COUSCOUS

Roast Lamb

Lamb shoulder roast,
   approximately 5 lb
2 Tbsp olive oil
½ cup Moroccan Spice Mix
   (see Moroccan-Spiced Sour Cherry
   preserves, page 38)
2 cups red wine

1 cup beef or veal stock
¼ cup sherry vinegar
½ cup chopped dates
½ cup chopped pistachios
¼ cup dried cherries
½ cup preserves (suggestions on
   next page)

1. Rub lamb shoulder with olive oil, then rub all over with ½ cup Moroccan Spice Mix. Cover and marinate for a minimum of two hours or overnight in the fridge.
2. The next day, bring lamb to room temperature for 30 minutes. Preheat oven to 325°F.
3. Transfer lamb to a large roasting pan and add wine, stock and vinegar to the pan. Cover with foil and place in the oven for 2½ hours.
4. Remove foil and add dates, pistachios, cherries and preserves to pan juices. Re-cover with foil and cook an additional 1 to 1½ hours until lamb is tender.
5. Remove meat from the pan and pour pan juices into a saucepan. Bring to a simmer and reduce for 15 to 20 minutes while meat is resting.
6. Carve meat and serve with couscous and pan sauce.

(recipe continues on next page)

(continued from previous page)

Moroccan Couscous

1 Tbsp olive oil

½ cup chopped onion

2 cloves garlic, minced

½ tsp salt

½ tsp ground cinnamon

½ tsp ground cumin

½ tsp ground coriander

¼ tsp ground ginger

2 cups couscous

2 cups fresh orange juice

½ cup raisins

½ cup chopped dried apricots

Zest and juice of 1 lemon

½ cup slivered almonds for garnish

¼ cup chopped cilantro for garnish

1. Heat a large saucepan over medium-high heat. Add oil to the hot pan and sauté onions and garlic. Add salt and spices and continue cooking until onions are nicely caramelized, about 3 to 5 minutes.

2. Add couscous, orange juice, raisins, apricots and lemon zest and juice and bring to a simmer. Reduce heat, cover and cook until couscous is tender, about 20 minutes.

3. Serve with lamb and garnish with almonds and cilantro.

❧

THREE PERFECT PRESERVES:

Moroccan-Spiced Sour Cherry, 38 | *Rainier Cherry & Kirsch, 41*

Apricot with Tarragon & Riesling, 48

{ SERVES FOUR }

Duck is one of those meats we often forget about, but it's simple to cook and so rich that you'll feel like you've had a nice steak (at least that's what I tell the carnivores in our house). The sauce is acidic enough to balance the richness of the duck. Chef Tina Fineza, a beautiful soul who lost her brave fight with cancer, is the inspiration for this dish, and Tina's quote, "Live how you want to be remembered," is one I love. I recommend going all in and serving it like Tina did after a visit to our farm, with a side of duck fat–fried potatoes and a simple cauliflower purée.

PAN-SEARED DUCK BREAST

4 duck breasts
Salt and pepper
2 shallots, sliced
1 clove garlic, minced

1 Tbsp fresh thyme
½ cup red wine
3 Tbsp port or D'oro
    fortified walnut wine

2 Tbsp balsamic vinegar
Zest and juice of 1
    medium orange
½ cup preserves
    (suggestions below)

1. Preheat oven to 350°F.
2. Crosshatch duck skin and season with salt and pepper. Place breasts skin side down in a cold, dry skillet. Place skillet on medium-low heat and sear until duck fat is rendered and crispy brown, about 15 to 20 minutes; do not turn over.
3. Place breasts skin side up on a baking sheet and finish in the oven for 10 to 15 minutes, until the internal temperature of the duck is 125°F to 130°F for medium-rare or 140°F for medium.
4. While duck is in the oven, drain out all but 1 Tbsp of the fat in your pan. (Reserve the remaining fat; you'll thank me later!) Sauté shallots, garlic and thyme in duck fat until caramelized. Deglaze pan with red wine, port and vinegar, then simmer and reduce for 5 minutes. Stir in orange zest and juice and preserves; continue simmering sauce until duck is ready.
5. Remove duck from the oven and rest 5 minutes before slicing. Ladle pan sauce over sliced duck.

❧

THREE PERFECT PRESERVES:
Moroccan-Spiced Sour Cherry, 38 | *Crabapple with Orange & Aperol, 69*
Kumquat with Vanilla & Vodka, 97

{SERVES SIX TO EIGHT}

This is a perfect meal for entertaining, as it can be made ahead. Reheat baked ham and serve along with cheddar biscuits later in the night when your guests are ready for a little filler. The "jammy" baked beans are deliciously old-fashioned and so great for a buffet. You can use the same preserve for both the ham and beans, or you can mix it up and get crazy with combos—your choice!

GLAZED COUNTRY HAM & JAM-BAKED BEANS

Glazed Country Ham
½ cup white wine
5 lb bone-in country ham

Glaze
1 cup preserves (suggestions below)
2 Tbsp grainy Dijon

1. Preheat oven to 325°F.
2. Whisk glaze ingredients together.
3. Pour wine over ham and bake for 30 minutes. Remove from oven and spread half the glaze mixture evenly over ham, reserving the remainder to serve alongside. Return to oven and cook until ham is heated through and internal temperature reaches 160°F, approximately 1½ hours. Rest ham for about 15 to 20 minutes before carving.
4. Serve with remaining glaze and Jam-Baked Beans.

Jam-Baked Beans
1 medium onion, chopped
1 Tbsp unsalted butter
1 tsp salt
1 cup preserves (suggestions below)
½ cup white wine vinegar
½ tsp Dijon
Four 14-oz cans navy beans, drained and rinsed

1. Sauté onion in butter, season with salt and cook until beginning to brown. Stir in preserves, vinegar and Dijon; bring just to a simmer.
2. Pour over beans in a greased ovenproof casserole dish and mix well. Bake alongside ham for about 1 hour.

THREE PERFECT PRESERVES:
Apricot with Tarragon & Riesling, 48 | Heritage Apple with Bacon & Scotch, 73 | Mulled Wine Jelly, 102

Pizzam with Beet with Oranges & Pink Peppercorn preserve (recipe page 186)

I promise you will never look at a pizza in the same way after you have tried a Pizzam! My husband, Patrick, and I shared some interesting flatbreads while on a quick trip to Whistler, British Columbia. That led to us thinking about making flatbreads for picnics at Vista D'oro, as well as the deliciously dressed up pizzas we had eaten at the market in Uzès in Provence, and the result of all this was pizzams. Just try one. The following is a base recipe for creating your own pizzams—use the suggested combinations on page 186, the Pizzam Party Plan on page 188 or let your imagination and pantry guide you.

PIZZAMS

Frozen pizza dough, thawed (or make your own—so simple!)
1 cup preserves (suggestions on next page)
½ cup chosen protein
½ cup crumbled or shredded cheese
½ cup chopped desired garnish
1 Tbsp olive oil (optional)

1. Season and heat a grill pan or barbecue.
2. Divide pizza dough into small rounds and roll out on a lightly floured surface.
3. Grill one side of each Pizzam crust; remove from grill onto a parchment-lined baking sheet, grilled side up. Top grilled side with preserves, protein and cheese.
4. Return to grill, ungrilled side down. Once cheese is melted and crust is nicely crisp, about 5 to 10 minutes, remove from grill, top with chosen garnish and drizzle with olive oil if desired—et voilà!

SUGGESTED PIZZAM COMBINATIONS

Heirloom Tomato & Chile (page 66), bocconcini, fresh tomatoes, radicchio, basil

Apricot with Tarragon & Riesling (page 48), duck confit, Oka, endive, fresh tarragon

Beet with Oranges & Pink Peppercorn (page 81), chèvre, mint, balsamic glaze

Heritage Apple with Bacon & Scotch (page 73), Gorgonzola, fried egg, frisée

Sweet Corn with Espelette & Chardonnay (page 65), scallops, bacon lardon, Gruyère, chives

Pineapple with Mint & Chile (page 106), pork belly, pecorino, scallions

Tomatillo & Chile (page 90), prawns, queso fresco, grilled poblano, avocado, cilantro

Spicy Sweet Charred Onion & Figs (page 86), mushrooms, Oka, arugula

Blueberry & French Thyme (page 44), grilled salmon, bocconcini, radicchio

Spiced Walnut Butter (page 116), *Plum with Vanilla & Star Anise* (page 58),
pancetta, bocconcini

Fig with Honey & Star Anise (page 62), prosciutto, blue cheese, arugula, fresh figs

Olive with Orange & Lemon (page 93), truffle salami,
Camembert, frisée (dressed), candied walnut

Pizzam Party Plan

Nothing beats a build-your-own pizza party, except a build-your-own Pizzam party! Invite the fun friends, the ones who like to eat with their fingers and love all things food. Summertime is the best time: picnic blankets and BBQs! Make it a BYOCB (craft beer), mix up some Jamargaritas (page 235), set up a Pizzam filling station, crank the funk and you're all set!

PIZZAM FILLING STATION

Preserves

Heirloom Tomato & Chile (page 66)

Indian-Spiced Green Tomato (page 89)

Chile Pepper (page 82)

Apricot with Tarragon & Riesling (page 48)

Beet with Oranges & Pink Peppercorn (page 81)

Sweet Corn with Espelette & Chardonnay (page 65)

Heritage Apple with Bacon & Scotch (page 73)

Proteins

Cooked sausage meat (pork, chicken, salmon)

Sliced salami

Prosciutto

Shredded duck confit (see page 159)

Raw peeled prawns

Sliced braised pork belly (see page 147)

Lightly seared scallops

(they'll finish cooking on the Pizzam)

Cheeses

Bocconcini (mini)

Gruyère

Aged cheddar

Camembert

Queso fresco

Stilton

Münster

Chèvre

Garnishes

Dressed greens

(frisée, radicchio, endive, arugula)

Fresh herbs (cilantro, mint, basil)

Fresh tomatoes, chopped

Grilled peppers, chopped

Chile peppers, finely chopped

Balsamic glaze

Olive oil

Truffle oil

Finishing salts

DESSERT

Oh, how I love thee! You may have guessed by now that I have a bit of an issue with sugar—there's a reason jam is my accidental career! I have vivid childhood memories of stealing a teaspoon of icing sugar from the baking cupboard and hiding in a closet to eat it . . . slowly! I cannot end a meal without a sweet treat. No matter how full I am, there is *always* room for dessert. My friends love going out with me; they can feel all saintly and not order dessert, as they can be assured that I will—and they inevitably have their "sharing" forks ready when mine arrives.

When I first decided I wanted to belong to this crazy food life, I desperately wanted to be a pastry chef. I figured out that it wasn't that I wanted to bake; I just wanted to eat the results!

As you can imagine, testing the recipes in this chapter was AWESOME! My favorite of the bunch is the Glazed Almond & Polenta Cake; it's perfect for breakfast and dessert. Enjoy!

DESSERT

{SERVES EIGHT TO TEN}

This traditional Italian dessert is lovely any time of day. I love the crunch of the polenta, the richness of the almond and the moist deliciousness that the preserves add to the mix.

GLAZED ALMOND & POLENTA CAKE

1 cup unsalted butter, softened

1 cup sugar

3 eggs

1 tsp vanilla extract

2 cups finely ground almonds

¾ cup coarse-ground cornmeal

1 tsp baking powder

½ tsp salt

Zest and juice of 2 medium oranges

2 cups preserves (suggestions below)

1. Preheat the oven to 325°F. Grease a 9-inch springform pan and line with parchment.

2. Cream butter and sugar together until light and fluffy. Add eggs, one at a time, to butter mixture; add vanilla just to incorporate.

3. Combine ground almonds, cornmeal, baking powder and salt in a separate bowl. Add dry mix to butter and egg mixture; mix until fully combined. Stir in orange zest.

4. Pour mixture into prepared pan and smooth the top. Bake 40 to 50 minutes until sides begin to pull away and a tester comes out with just a few crumbs attached.

5. Meanwhile, in a small saucepan, combine orange juice and preserves. Heat to simmer and keep warm.

6. Remove cake from oven and prick the surface all over with a toothpick. Pour the warm preserve mixture over the hot cake and cool.

❧

THREE PERFECT PRESERVES:

Blood Orange with Coconut & Lillet, 101 | *Seville Orange with Cardamom & Brandy, 110*

Apricot with Tarragon & Riesling, 48

This is one of those great make-ahead desserts that impresses, yet is deceptively simple to prepare. The layer of preserves is so pretty, you'll want to make this in glass containers. As it happens, jam jars are perfect! If you have the patience, you can make this in two batches to produce layers; if not, simply put the preserves on the bottom.

BUTTERMILK PANNA COTTA

6 to 8 Tbsp preserves
 (suggestions below)
1 Tbsp powdered gelatin
¼ cup cold water

½ cup heavy cream
¼ cup sugar
Seeds from one vanilla bean
1½ cups buttermilk

1. Lightly butter or apply nonstick spray to six to eight 4-oz ramekins or jam jars. Place 1 Tbsp preserves in each and set aside.
2. In a small bowl, mix gelatin into cold water and let sit for about 10 minutes to bloom.
3. Combine cream, sugar and seeds from the vanilla bean in a saucepan over medium heat. Carefully heat to a low simmer, stirring constantly to dissolve sugar. Remove from heat and stir in gelatin mixture. Add buttermilk and stir to combine into warm cream.
4. Cool slightly, then strain the mixture. Pour the strained cream, carefully, over preserves in the ramekins. Refrigerate 4 hours to set.

THREE PERFECT PRESERVES:

Rhubarb & Vanilla, 29 | *Rainier Cherry & Kirsch, 41* | *Strawberry & Roses, 34*

{MAKES ONE 9-INCH ROUND CHEESECAKE OR SIX 4-INCH RING-MOLD CHEESECAKES}

The only thing better than cheesecake is more cheesecake. This is great to serve as part of a dessert buffet; it's almost a cheese course, really. One base, three versions of delicious cheesecake—make just one or all three, depending on your crowd and/or hunger. The technique is the same for all three versions, although I have to admit, I'm weak for the blue cheese version; with the Fig with Honey & Star Anise preserve, it is out of this world.

CHEESECAKE TRIO

Graham Cracker Base

1½ cups graham cracker crumbs

3 Tbsp sugar

⅓ cup unsalted butter, melted

Goat Cheese Filling

1½ cups soft goat cheese

1½ cups cream cheese, softened

1 cup sugar

3 eggs

Preserves (suggestions below)

French Vanilla Filling

3 cups cream cheese, softened

1 cup sugar

3 eggs

1 vanilla bean, seeds scraped into eggs

Preserves (suggestions below)

Blue Cheese Filling

1 cup crumbled blue cheese

2 cups cream cheese, softened

1 cup sugar

3 eggs

Preserves (suggestions below)

1. Combine all base ingredients and press into the bottom of a 9-inch springform pan or six 4-inch ring molds.
2. Preheat oven to 300°F.
3. Blend cheese(s) and sugar until well combined. Add eggs, one at a time, until well incorporated. (If you are making the French vanilla, scrape the vanilla bean seeds into the eggs first.)
4. For all three versions, pour mixture onto prepared graham crust base and bake for 30 to 35 minutes for one 9-inch cheesecake, or 20 to 25 minutes for the 4-inch cheesecakes, or until almost set in the middle. Let cool one hour, then spread with preserves, cool completely and refrigerate for 4 hours or overnight before slicing.

THREE PERFECT PRESERVES:

Goat cheese: Raspberry with Merlot & Peppercorn, 43 | *French vanilla: Smoked Lime Margarita, 105*

Blue cheese: Fig with Honey & Star Anise, 62

{MAKES ONE 9-INCH LAYER CAKE}

The additions of buttermilk and sour cream make this one of the moistest chocolate cakes ever. The preserves also help keep the layers ultra-moist. Raspberry with Merlot & Peppercorn pairs beautifully with the chocolate and Rainier Cherry & Kirsch turns it into a decadent version of Black Forest cake; so many other preserves work wonderfully in this dessert as well.

CHOCOLATE LAYER CAKE

3 cups all-purpose flour

2½ cups sugar

1½ cups cocoa powder

1¼ tsp salt

1 Tbsp baking powder

1 Tbsp baking soda

5 large eggs

1 Tbsp vanilla extract

1 cup buttermilk

½ cup sour cream

¾ cup unsalted butter, melted

1½ cups strong coffee or espresso, warm

1 cup preserves (suggestions below)

Chocolate Mocha Ganache (recipe opposite) or your favorite classic buttercream frosting (pictured)

Fresh fruit for garnish (optional)

1. Preheat oven to 350°F. Grease and flour two 9-inch round cake pans.

2. Whisk dry ingredients together in a large mixing bowl. In a smaller bowl, whisk eggs and vanilla, then combine into the dry mixture. Incorporate the buttermilk, sour cream, melted butter, and coffee into the batter. Divide batter evenly into the prepared pans.

3. Bake 30 to 40 minutes, until tester comes out clean. Cool cakes on a rack and remove from pans once cool enough to handle.

4. To assemble, slice each cake in half horizontally. Spread ⅓ cup of preserves evenly on three of the cake rounds. If using buttercream, spread a layer on top of the preserves. Stack the layers, with the last layer having no preserves on the top. If you like, pour warm ganache evenly over the cake or frost cake with buttercream. Garnish with fresh fruit.

THREE PERFECT PRESERVES:

Pear & Cocoa Nib, 78 | *Raspberry with Merlot & Peppercorn, 43* | *Rainier Cherry & Kirsch, 41*

Chocolate Mocha Ganache

2 cups chopped dark chocolate
1 ½ cups whipping cream
3 Tbsp unsalted butter
1 ½ Tbsp instant espresso powder
2 Tbsp sugar

1. Place chocolate into a large stainless-steel bowl.
2. In a saucepan, heat remaining ingredients to a simmer, watching closely so the mixture doesn't boil over.
3. Pour hot cream mixture over chocolate, wait 2 minutes, then stir well with a spatula until chocolate is completely melted. Be sure to lick the spatula to determine if it's acceptable!

{MAKES ABOUT 3 DOZEN}

This is based on my Auntie Lu's recipe. Lu is in her 90s and is still making these every Christmas for the family. The hardest part is waiting for the batter to rise. Make sure you have a snack to hold you over, or you'll end up eating them hot right out of the fryer. (I'm just guessing that might happen. I have so much restraint, it would never happen to me . . . !)

FRITOLE

4 cups all-purpose flour	¾ cup warm water
1½ cups + 1 tsp sugar	3½ tsp active dry yeast
1 Tbsp cinnamon	½ cup chopped pecans or walnuts
1 tsp salt	¼ cup whiskey
1 cup preserves (suggestions below)	Canola oil for deep-frying
2 cups boiling water	Sugar or icing sugar for rolling

1. Whisk to combine flour, 1½ cups sugar, cinnamon and salt in a large mixing bowl.
2. Stir preserves into boiling water and, while still very hot, pour the mixture over the dry ingredients. Mix until quite easy to stir, adding more hot water if required. Cool to lukewarm.
3. In a small bowl, dissolve 1 tsp sugar in ¾ cup warm water. Sprinkle yeast into the bowl and let stand 10 minutes to activate the yeast. Stir yeast mixture into the batter, then stir in chopped nuts. Cover with a kitchen towel and let rise in a warm spot until doubled in size, 2 to 3 hours, or overnight in the fridge.
4. Once the dough has risen, gently stir in whiskey until fully incorporated.
5. Fill a heavy-bottomed pot with oil to about 3 inches. Heat oil to 350°F to 360°F. Using a teaspoon, carefully drop dough into the hot oil a few at a time. Turn carefully with tongs to brown evenly. Cook until dark golden brown, about 1 to 2 minutes. Drain on paper towels, then roll, while still warm, in sugar or cool slightly and dust with icing sugar. Repeat until all the batter is gone. Best served warm.

THREE PERFECT PRESERVES:

Heritage Apple with Bacon & Scotch, 73 | *Chestnut with Dates & Brandy, 100*
Persimmon with Cinnamon & Pecans, 109

{SERVES SIX TO EIGHT}

This is basically an even lazier version of pavlova, if that's possible. Eton Mess is a British school staple. An easy curd is not typically in an Eton Mess, but I love the addition. For a new dessert each time, change up the curd, preserves and garnish at will. My preferred combo is passion fruit curd, Plain Ol' Wild Blackberry (page 61) and a simple garnish of fresh mint.

ETON MESS

Meringue
4 egg whites
Pinch of salt
1 cup sugar

Curd
4 eggs
1½ cups sugar

½ cup juice
(blood orange,
passion fruit, lime or
lemon)
½ cup unsalted butter,
softened and cut into
8 pieces

1½ cups whipping
cream, whipped to
soft peaks
1 cup preserves
(suggestions below)
Fresh mint, chopped
nuts or cocoa powder
for garnish

1. To make the meringue, preheat oven to 250°F.
2. Whisk egg whites in a stand mixer or by hand in a large stainless steel bowl until foamy. Add a pinch of salt and continue whisking while slowly adding in sugar. Whisk until stiff and glossy peaks form. Spread meringue out on parchment-lined baking sheet to about ¾-inch thickness. Bake until dry and cream-colored, about 1 hour. Cool and break meringue into small bite-sized chunks.
3. To make the curd, fill medium saucepan with one inch of water and bring to a simmer. Whisk eggs and sugar in a stand mixer until light and thick. Pour in juice and place bowl over simmering water in the saucepan, being careful your bowl does not touch the water. Continue whisking by hand until mixture is thickened. Remove from heat and stir in pieces of butter, two at a time, until fully incorporated into curd. Cover and refrigerate.
4. To assemble, place a layer of broken meringue, curd, whipped cream and preserves in individual parfait glasses or in one large glass bowl. Repeat with two or three additional layers, then top with garnish.

THREE PERFECT PRESERVES:
Plain Ol' Wild Blackberry, 61 | Raspberry with Chocolate & Brandy, 43
Grilled Peach with Blackberry & Candied Ginger, 52

{MAKES SIX 4-INCH TARTS OR ONE 9-INCH CROSTATA}

This is a traditional Italian dessert, like a light rustic cheesecake, that is not overly sweet (we won't hold that against it) and that is equally good for breakfast. This keeps well for a few days well wrapped in the fridge—if you can resist eating it for that long.

RICOTTA & JAM CROSTATA

Super-Forgiving Italian Dough—*Pasta Frolla*

2 cups all-purpose flour	½ tsp baking powder	½ cup cold butter
⅓ cup sugar	¼ tsp salt	2 eggs, lightly beaten

Ricotta Filling

2 cups ricotta
(see Ricotta Toast, page 117, for homemade, or store-bought works just as well)

Zest of 1 lemon	¼ cup sugar	½ cup preserves,
Zest of 1 small orange	3 eggs	warmed (suggestions below)

1. To make the pastry dough, whisk dry ingredients together. Grate cold butter over dry mixture and rub with your fingers to incorporate well. Pour eggs into dough and mix well to combine to form a ball. Knead 1 to 2 minutes, then wrap in plastic wrap, flatten and chill for 30 minutes.
2. Preheat oven to 350°F.
3. Whisk together ricotta, citrus zests, sugar and eggs until well blended.
4. Roll out pastry and line individual tart shells or a 9-inch tart pan; freeze any leftover pastry for another time or use for Jam Tartlettes (page 211). Pour warm preserves over pastry and spread to all edges. Pour ricotta filling over preserves and smooth top with a spatula.
5. Bake until the crust is golden and the filling is set, 20 to 30 minutes for the 4-inch tarts or 35 to 45 minutes for the 9-inch.

THREE PERFECT PRESERVES:

Blood Orange with Coconut & Lillet, 101 | *Rhubarb with Ginger & Orange Zest, 31*
Peach with Lemon Verbena & Champagne, 55

{SERVES SIX}

This old-school dessert originated in Great Britain. I had it while in London at St. John Bar & Restaurant, and I don't know why it's not on more menus. It's the perfect balance of gooey goodness—kind of a bread pudding meets lemon meringue pie. Serve this hot from the oven, with a perfect pot of tea fit for a queen.

QUEEN OF PUDDINGS

Custardy Cake Base
2 tsp unsalted butter

2 cups fresh bread crumbs, made from fresh white bread, crusts removed

2 cups whole milk

¼ cup sugar

1 Tbsp lemon or orange zest

3 egg yolks

Meringue
4 egg whites

⅓ cup sugar

1 tsp vanilla extract

1 cup preserves (suggestions below)

¼ cup unsweetened shredded coconut

1. Preheat oven to 325°F.

2. Butter six 4-inch individual ramekins or one 9-inch ceramic baking dish and spread bread crumbs evenly over the bottom.

3. Heat milk, butter, sugar and zest in a saucepan over medium-high heat until sugar has dissolved.

4. Whisk egg yolks in a large stainless-steel bowl, then very slowly whisk warm milk mixture into eggs.

5. Pour warm mixture over bread crumbs in the dish. Let the liquid absorb into the bread crumbs for about 10 minutes.

6. Bake until custard is set, about 20 minutes. Remove and cool.

7. Meanwhile, prepare meringue by whisking egg whites until beginning to foam. Slowly add in sugar while continuing to whisk. Beat until stiff and shiny, then whisk in vanilla to combine.

8. Spread a thick layer of warmed preserves evenly over the cooled base, then pipe or spoon meringue over top and sprinkle with coconut. Place back in the oven and bake until meringue is evenly golden, about 3 to 5 minutes.

❧

THREE PERFECT PRESERVES:

Strawberry & Roses, 34 | *Pear & Cocoa Nib, 78* | *Chestnut with Dates & Brandy, 100*

THREE PERFECT PRESERVE AND FRUIT COMBINATIONS WITH FRANGIPANE:

Peach with Lemon Verbena & Champagne (page 55); fresh raspberries

Rainier Cherry & Kirsch (page 41); fresh orange segments

Rhubarb with Ginger & Orange Zest (page 31); fresh pomegranate seeds

THREE PERFECT PRESERVE AND NUT COMBINATIONS WITHOUT FRANGIPANE:

Strawberry with Pistachio & Vanilla (page 32); chopped pistachios

Sweet Potato Pie (page 85); chopped candied pecans

Raspberry with Chocolate & Brandy (page 43); slivered almonds

{MAKES 10 TO 12 3-INCH TARTLETTES}

These little gems are perfect for tea parties—or, if you keep a little extra tart dough in your freezer, for last-minute dinner guests. The frangipane is optional, but adds a lovely orangey-almond touch. You can also use the pastry recipe from page 206 in place of the tartlette pastry below. Flavor combinations are only suggestions. Use your creativity and let your jam-freak flag fly!

JAM TARTLETTES

Tartlette Pastry

2 cups all-purpose flour	1 tsp salt	5 Tbsp sour cream
2 tsp sugar	1 cup cold butter	⅔ cup ice water

Frangipane (optional)

1 cup almond paste	1 Tbsp orange zest	1 cup preserves
¼ cup sugar	¼ tsp salt	(suggestions opposite)
⅓ cup butter, softened	2 eggs	Fruit and chopped nuts
1 tsp vanilla extract	⅓ cup all-purpose flour	for garnish

1. In a large mixing bowl, whisk together flour, sugar and salt. Cut in cold butter with a pastry cutter or grate in with a large-hole grater (much quicker and easier). Rub the butter and flour mixture gently with your fingers to combine until butter pieces are about ¼ inch in size.

2. Whisk sour cream and ice water together and add to dry ingredients, stirring just until combined. Gather into a ball, knead 2 to 3 times only and press into a flat disc. Wrap in plastic wrap and chill for at least 30 minutes.

3. If using frangipane, combine all ingredients in a mixing bowl until well incorporated.

4. Preheat oven to 375°F.

5. Roll out pastry dough to about ⅛-inch thickness, cut into rounds and place in 3-inch tart molds. Fill with a layer of frangipane, if using, and preserves.

6. Bake until edges are golden, approximately 15 minutes. Garnish tarts with fresh contrasting fruit or chopped nuts (see suggestions opposite).

{ SERVES SIX TO EIGHT }

Rich, jammy, chocolatey: the holy trinity of what a dessert should be. A day-old loaf of brioche is perfect for this decadent bread pudding, and you can prepare this the night before and bake an hour before you're serving. I also love bread pudding with a big cup of coffee for breakfast.

BREAD PUDDING WITH CHOCOLATE & JAM

1½ cups whole milk
1½ cups cream
Seeds from one vanilla bean
3 eggs
3 egg yolks

½ cup sugar
Pinch of salt
1 loaf of brioche, sliced and quartered
1½ cups preserves (suggestions below)
1 cup chopped good dark chocolate

1. Preheat oven to 325°F. Butter an 8-inch square glass baking dish.
2. Layer brioche with chocolate and preserves in prepared dish.
3. In a medium saucepan, combine milk, cream and vanilla seeds over medium heat. Bring just to a simmer and remove from heat.
4. In a large mixing bowl, whisk eggs, yolks, sugar and salt. Slowly whisk warm milk mixture into eggs until fully incorporated.
5. Pour mixture into prepared baking dish. Bake until custard is set, 20 to 30 minutes. Best served warm or toast leftovers for breakfast.

❦

THREE PERFECT PRESERVES:
Banana with Passion Fruit & Rum, 98 | *Raspberry with Chocolate & Brandy, 43* | *Pear & Cocoa Nib, 78*

CHEESE, CHARCUTERIE, PICKLES & COCKTAILS

My obsession with cheese started in earnest, not surprisingly, on my first trip to Paris. I stopped in at a very small, smelly and jam-packed—pun intended—*fromagerie* for a piece of Brie. My French was and still is *très mauvais,* and the lovely madam in the white lab coat behind the counter posed a litany of questions that I had no hope of understanding. After some charades and broken English on her side and broken French on mine, I determined that she needed to know what time (not day) I would be serving the Brie. That is how seriously the French take their cheese.

As for pork products and preserves: a match made in heaven! While not all charcuterie is pork-based, much of it is. Sweet preserves and acidic pickles are what tie a great charcuterie board together—that, and a good hunk of bread.

Pickles very nearly got their own chapter. Let's just say that I think I have found a new hobby.

And last, but never least, a few jam-filled cocktails. It starts innocently enough, with a teaspoon of jam added to a cocktail shaker, and before you know it your bar setup isn't complete without a few jars of preserves. Cheers!

CHEESE, CHARCUTERIE, PICKLES & COCKTAILS

CHEESE

One of my proudest moments as a cook was preparing the cheese course at Julia Child's 100th birthday gala in Vancouver. The annual event, hosted by Les Dames d'Escoffier, of which I'm a member, featured ten chefs and ten courses. I was so nervous about my course, my friend and fellow Dame, Stephanie, had her husband, Chef Scott Jaeger of the Pear Tree Restaurant in Vancouver, talk me through. I ended up with a beautiful plate, thanks to Scott's mentoring.

Charles de Gaulle famously said, "How can you govern a country which has 246 varieties of cheese?" I felt his pain choosing my favorites for the cheese chart on the following page, which gives pairings for all the preserves in this book and is offered as a guideline. Below are some of my suggestions for a perfect cheese board.

FAVORITE ARTISAN PRODUCERS

BRITISH COLUMBIA
- *Farm House Natural Cheeses*—Alpine Gold and Clothbound Cheddar
- *Salt Spring Island Cheese Company*—Truffle Chèvre
- *Moonstruck Cheese*—White Grace
- *Poplar Grove Cheese*—Tiger Blue
- *Golden Ears Cheesecrafters*—Fenugreek Gouda

CALIFORNIA
- *Cowgirl Creamery*—Mt Tam
- *Cypress Grove*—Purple Haze and Humboldt Fog

OREGON
- *Rogue Creamery*—Oregon Blue

IMPORTED FAVORITES

Cave-aged Gruyère	*Comté*
Burrata	*Brillat-Savarin*
Délice de Bourgogne	*Bresse Bleu*
Saint Agur	*Pecorino*
Le Dauphin	*Piave Vecchio*
Saint-André	*Manchego*

OTHER CHEESE BOARD NICETIES

Lesley Stowe's Raincoast Crisps	*Breadsticks*
La Panzanella Croccantini	*Fresh baguette*
Good mix of toasted nuts	*or pain de campagne*
Dried fruit	*Honeycomb*
Fresh fruit	

	HARD CHEESES						SOFT CHEESES				
	Cave-Aged Gruyère	Comté	Piave	Clothbound Cheddar	Parmigiano-Reggiano		Saint-André	Délice de Bourgogne	Brillat-Savarin	Le Dauphin	Brie/Camembert
Rhubarb & Vanilla	•			•				•	•	•	•
Rhubarb with Ginger & Orange Zest							•				
Strawberry with Pistachio & Vanilla		•					•		•		
Strawberry & Roses					•		•	•			•
Roasted Strawberry & Mint											
Moroccan-Spiced Sour Cherry		•									
Raspberry with Merlot & Peppercorn									•	•	
Raspberry with Chocolate & Brandy											
Blueberry & French Thyme	•							•			
Rainier Cherry & Kirsch	•	•	•	•	•					•	•
Apricot with Tarragon & Riesling	•		•	•				•			•
Damson Plum & Sweet Vermouth	•	•	•	•				•		•	
Grilled Peach with Blackberry & Candied Ginger											•
Peach with Lemon Verbena & Champagne											
Plum with Vanilla & Star Anise	•		•	•			•			•	•
Plain Ol' Wild Blackberry				•				•	•		•
Fig with Honey & Star Anise	•	•	•	•	•		•	•	•	•	•
Sweet Corn with Espelette & Chardonnay											
Heirloom Tomato & Chile				•			•			•	
Crabapple with Orange & Aperol											
Heritage Apple with Bacon & Scotch		•					•				
Pear & Vanilla Bean	•							•	•		•
Pear & Cocoa Nib		•									
Beet with Oranges & Pink Peppercorn					•					•	•
Chile Pepper											
Sweet Potato Pie											
Spicy Sweet Charred Onion & Figs	•		•	•	•						•
Indian-Spiced Green Tomato	•			•							
Tomatillo & Chile											
Olive with Orange & Lemon	•		•	•	•						
Kumquat with Vanilla & Vodka							•	•			•
Chestnut with Dates & Brandy		•					•		•		
Banana with Passion Fruit & Rum		•									
Blood Orange with Coconut & Lillet		•					•				
Mulled Wine Jelly			•		•						
Smoked Lime Margarita											
Piña Colada											
Persimmon with Cinnamon & Pecans	•	•		•	•		•			•	•
Seville Orange with Cardamom & Brandy								•			
Pineapple with Mint & Chile											

	BLUE CHEESES					GOAT & SHEEP'S MILK CHEESES					WASHED RIND & OTHER CHEESES					
	Roquefort	Gorgonzola	Saint Agur	Bleu de Bresse	Stilton	Chèvre	Manchego	Crottin de Chavignol	Pecorino	Humboldt Fog	Epoisses	Munster	Ricotta	Mascarpone	Smoked Gouda	Queso Fresco
		•	•		•			•	•		•		•		•	
	•						•		•				•			•
						•							•	•		
						•		•		•	•	•				
		•							•				•	•		•
		•					•			•					•	•
						•		•		•		•				
													•	•		
	•		•					•	•				•			
		•	•			•	•				•		•			
	•			•		•	•	•								
		•				•		•	•				•	•		•
						•							•	•		
							•	•	•		•		•			
		•					•		•			•			•	
	•						•	•	•		•		•	•		•
	•			•	•		•	•	•	•	•		•	•	•	
									•				•			•
									•				•	•		
							•			•	•		•			•
							•				•			•		
		•						•		•	•	•			•	
									•				•	•		
						•		•		•		•	•		•	•
						•							•			•
		•					•								•	
			•	•				•	•				•		•	
						•				•	•		•			•
									•				•			•
						•			•				•		•	
						•	•			•	•		•	•		
		•					•			•		•	•		•	
							•						•			•
									•				•	•		•
								•					•		•	
						•							•			•
						•							•			•
		•		•	•		•		•				•		•	
								•					•			
					•	•										•

{ONE DOZEN}

A simple little bite to start the night! A great addition to salads or served alongside pâté.

Top these savory shortbread-like crackers with your favorite preserve. Perfect served with Prosecco!

CRISPY CHEESE DISCS

2 cups grated Parmesan or aged Gouda (or any really flavorful cheese)
2 Tbsp all-purpose flour
1 Tbsp freshly ground pepper

1. Stir ingredients with a fork to combine.
2. Heat a non-stick frying pan over medium-high heat. Spoon cheese mixture into small piles evenly in the hot pan. Brown on both sides, approximately 2 minutes per side. You can also do these on a parchment-lined baking sheet baked in a 375°F oven for 5 to 7 minutes until crispy.
3. Cool discs on rack and serve with your favorite preserves!

WALNUT & BLUE CHEESE CRACKERS

1 cup walnuts, toasted at 350°F for 10 to 15 minutes and finely ground
1 cup all-purpose flour
2 Tbsp coarse ground black pepper
6 Tbsp cold unsalted butter
7 Tbsp crumbled soft blue cheese
2 Tbsp flaked sea salt (I like Maldon)

1. Whisk together ground walnuts, flour and pepper. Cut in cold butter, or use a cheese grater (even easier!). Rub mixture with your fingers just to combine. Add in blue cheese and mix until a dough forms.
2. Shape into a log and wrap in parchment, and refrigerate for 2 hours. (Logs will keep for up to 3 days in the fridge or for 3 months in the freezer.)
3. To bake crackers, preheat oven to 325°F. Slice the chilled log into ¼-inch slices and place on a parchment-lined baking sheet. Sprinkle with sea salt and bake until slightly browned, 20 to 30 minutes or longer if baking from frozen. Transfer to a rack to cool. These keep well in an airtight container for up to 4 days.
4. Serve topped with preserves.

{MAKES APPROXIMATELY 2 DOZEN 1-INCH OATCAKES}

Grandma Gracie kept a tin of bacon grease beside the stove year-round. My food safety brain won't allow me to do this, so I use fresh bacon grease, and I highly recommend you do the same! You could simply use olive oil, but the flavor won't be anywhere near as decadent.

GRANDMA GRACIE'S SCOTTISH OATCAKES

1 cup steel-cut oats
1 cup fine oatmeal
½ cup all-purpose flour
½ tsp salt
¼ cup warm bacon fat (see page 73)
1 tsp baking soda
¼ cup hot water
(plus more if necessary)

1. Preheat oven to 325°F.
2. Combine oats, oatmeal, flour and salt. Stir in warm bacon fat.
3. Dissolve baking soda in hot water and slowly add to the mixture. Use enough hot water to make a stiff dough, adding a bit less or more as necessary.
4. Roll out dough on floured surface and cut into rounds. Place on parchment-lined baking sheet and bake for approximately 10 minutes, until the oatcakes are beginning to brown.
5. Serve smeared with butter and a dollop of preserves.

THREE PERFECT PRESERVES:
Heritage Apple with Bacon & Scotch, 73 | *Persimmon with Cinnamon & Pecans, 109*
Apricot with Tarragon & Riesling, 48

CHARCUTERIE

Here is a quick guide to creating the perfect, groaning charcuterie board.

CHARCUTERIE

Lardo	*Saucisson sec*	*Coppa*
Pepperoni	*Truffle and duck pâté*	*Duck pistachio terrine*
Prosciutto	*Duck prosciutto*	*Soppressata*
Finocchiona salami	*Jamón ibérico*	*Dried chorizo*
Hot capicola	*Rosette de Lyon*	*Speck*
Bresaola	*Campagne Parisienne*	*Foie gras terrine*

PRESERVES FOR CHARCUTERIE

Moroccan-Spiced Sour Cherry, 38
Damson Plum & Sweet Vermouth, 51
Plum with Vanilla & Star Anise, 58
Spicy Sweet Charred Onion & Figs, 86
Olive with Orange & Lemon, 93
Persimmon with Cinnamon & Pecans, 109

OTHER ACCOUTREMENTS

Pickles
Mustards (grainy Dijon or flavored)
Maldon flaked sea salt
Freshly cracked pepper
Lesley Stowe's Raincoast Crisps
La Panzanella Croccantini
Dried fruit
Olives or tapenade
Breadsticks
Rustic artisan breads

PICKLES

Apparently pickling is almost as addictive as jam-making, and you can be as creative once you get started. The lineup of jars in my test kitchen is so beautiful with all the colors and textures. Don't be afraid to experiment. This basic sweet brine recipe works just as well with balsamic, pear, red or white wine, sherry or apple cider vinegar. Substitute demerara sugar for plain sugar, or try a flavored salt . . . there are so many options. Feel free to double or quadruple these base recipes at will!

{YIELDS ENOUGH FOR ONE 16-OZ/500-ML JAR}

BASIC SWEET BRINE RECIPE

1¼ cups vinegar

½ cup water

1 cup sugar

1 Tbsp kosher salt

1. Combine brine ingredients in a stainless steel pot. Bring to a boil and keep hot while preparing your veggies and jars.

STANDARD STEPS FOR PICKLING

1. Prep your veggies or fruit (ensure you have enough to pack jar tightly); wash and chop into bite size (ish) pieces.
2. Gather other add-in ingredients, such as spices, herbs, chilies.
3. Heat clean jars in a 225°F oven for 30 minutes and lids for 15 minutes to sterilize.
4. Pack hot jars with veggies and add-ins.
5. Pour hot brine over veggies to fill up to ¼ inch from the top of each jar.
6. Place hot lid on, flip jar upside down and cool. Pickles are best after about two weeks, and stored in a dry dark space are good for up to one year. Refrigerate after opening.

These four were the winners after a long weekend of pickling. The Peppery Pickled Shallots are a perfect accompaniment for pâté, or on a roast beef sandwich. The Indian-Spiced Pickled Cauliflower has been on my mind literally for months. I like many others am obsessed with cauliflower, curried in particular. The Spicy Pickled Brussels Sprouts are so delicious . . . many a believer in Brussels sprouts it has made. We substituted demerara sugar for the plain sugar in the brine for the Pickled Young Carrots & Ginger, and I loved the depth of flavor it gave. Beautiful on a charcuterie board or simply straight out of the jar for a quick snack!

PEPPERY PICKLED SHALLOTS

Into Each Jar . . .

2 cups shallots, sliced
2 slices fresh ginger, peeled
2 pieces of orange peel
½ tsp pink peppercorns
½ tsp black peppercorns
½ tsp white peppercorns
½ tsp coriander seeds

INDIAN-SPICED PICKLED CAULIFLOWER

Into Each Jar . . .

2 cups cauliflower,
cut into bite-sized florets
1 whole chile
3 slices fresh ginger, peeled
1 tsp fenugreek
1 tsp black onion seeds
1 tsp Madras curry powder
2 pieces lime peel
2-inch piece lemongrass,
sliced vertically and quartered
2 fresh lime leaves

SPICY PICKLED BRUSSELS SPROUTS

Into Each Jar . . .

2 cups Brussels sprouts, halved
1 whole chile pepper
1 tsp coriander seeds
½ tsp mustard seeds
½ tsp whole peppercorns
2 garlic cloves, peeled

PICKLED YOUNG CARROTS & GINGER

Into Each Jar . . .

10-12 young carrots,
peeled and trimmed to fit jars
2 whole chile peppers
1 tsp coriander seeds
2 slices fresh ginger, peeled

{YIELDS FOUR 16-OZ/500-ML JARS}

I use quotes on the kimchi, as this is not a true version. Real kimchi is fermented to give it that distinctive sour funk. I add a bit of fish sauce as a quick replacement. Endive and radicchio are also not traditional—cabbage being the usual suspect. This recipe is quick and easy and produces a great condiment that you'll find more uses for than you'd ever think. Caryn, our head honcho at the Preservatory, recommended the overnight weighted step, as her grandma made a similar traditional Japanese version with sui choi. I love the end result! Try it over steamed rice, on a hot dog or in an Unlikely Reuben (recipe page 138).

ENDIVE & RADICCHIO "KIMCHI"

4 Belgian endive, chopped
3 heads of radicchio, chopped
2 Tbsp sugar
2 Tbsp salt
5 cloves garlic, peeled
5 two-inch slices fresh ginger, peeled
½ cup preserves (suggestions below)

¼ cup rice wine vinegar
2 Tbsp sesame seeds
2 Tbsp fish sauce
2 tsp sambal oelek or red chile paste
2 tsp soy sauce
5 green onions, chopped

1. Place endive, radicchio, sugar and salt in a colander set over a bowl, and combine well. Place another smaller bowl or plate over top with a weight to press the mixture overnight in the fridge.
2. The next day, rinse the salad mixture with clean water.
3. In a food processor, combine the remaining ingredients, other than the green onions. Whiz well to blend mixture. Pour over rinsed endive and radicchio, add chopped green onions and mix well to coat evenly (this is best done with your hands).
4. Pack tight into sterilized jars and keep refrigerated until ready to use. Keeps for 2 to 3 weeks.

THREE PERFECT PRESERVES:
Chile Pepper, 82 | *Tomatillo & Chile, 90* | *Pineapple with Mint & Chile, 106*

COCKTAILS

What better way to finish a book, or a long day on the farm, than with cocktails! We started innocently enough, adding preserves to our signature sangria, and that led to a martini party trick of adding a dollop of Rhubarb & Vanilla preserve to the shaker. Preserves can add a lovely depth of sweetness to your bartending repertoire. Salute!

{MAKES I PITCHER}

Yeah, I totally went there. This makes a pitcher; it's up to you to decide how many people you'll share it with. To blend or not to blend—I prefer mine stirred and poured over ice.

JAMARGARITAS

1½ cups tequila
½ cup preserves (suggestions below)
1 cup beer (I use a pale lager)
1 cup fresh lime juice
Fresh mint for garnish
Sliced fresh fruit for garnish (strawberries,
limes or pineapple)

1. Combine tequila, preserves, beer and lime juice in a large pitcher, stir well and add 1 cup of ice. Pour over more ice in short glasses and garnish with mint and fresh fruit, if you like.

❧

THREE PERFECT PRESERVES:
Roasted Strawberry & Mint, 37
Peach with Lemon Verbena & Champagne, 55
Smoked Lime Margarita (pictured), 105

{MAKES 1 COCKTAIL}

A sweet sparkling treat, perfect for baby showers, bachelorette parties or lazy days in bed!

KIR PRESERVE ROYALE

1 Tbsp preserves (suggestions below)   4 oz champagne or Prosecco

1. Carefully spoon preserves into the bottom of a champagne flute, top with champagne *et voilà!*

THREE PERFECT PRESERVES:
Crabapple with Orange & Aperol, 69 | *Roasted Strawberry & Mint, 37*
Peach with Lemon Verbena & Champagne, 55

You might be thinking that this sounds like a vanity project, and, well, quite frankly you'd be right. I have high hopes of seeing this on a cocktail list sometime in my future. A combination of my go-to cocktail and preserves sounds just about perfect to me!

LEE-GRONI

1 Tbsp preserves (suggestions below)   ¾ oz vermouth
1 ½ oz gin   Orange bitters
¾ oz Campari   Orange peel for garnish

1. Combine ingredients and stir well. Pour over ice into a short tumbler and garnish with orange peel.

THREE PERFECT PRESERVES:
Seville Orange with Cardamom & Brandy, 110 | *Blood Orange with Coconut & Lillet, 101*
Crabapple with Orange & Aperol, 69

Not sure if Bond would approve, but these are ridiculously delicious!

THE PRESERVATORY MARTINI

2 oz vodka or gin
(I prefer the latter, in case you're asking)
1 Tbsp preserves (suggestions below)
1 oz juice to match
(see suggested combinations below)

1. Combine all ingredients in a shaker with ice, give it a good shake and strain into a chilled martini glass.

THREE PERFECT PRESERVE
AND JUICE COMBINATIONS:

Rhubarb & Vanilla, 29; lemon juice
Kumquat with Vanilla & Vodka, 97; orange juice
Damson Plum & Sweet Vermouth, 51; lemon juice

The Preservatory Sangria
(see recipe on next page)

{MAKES 1 PITCHER}

Perfect after a long day of weeding, chasing loose horses or boring bookkeeping. You could even share this with friends!

THE PRESERVATORY SANGRIA

½ cup preserves
(suggestions below)
1 cup mint leaves
1 cup lemon verbena leaves
2 cups local, seasonal fruit,
such as berries, peaches
or cherries

1 medium orange, sliced
1 lemon, sliced
1 cup D'oro fortified
walnut wine (or port works
perfectly as well)

3 cups Vista D'oro Pinot
Noir, or any other light
Burgundy-style Pinot
(the better the wine,
the better the sangria!)
1 cup club soda

1.   In a large pitcher, muddle preserves with mint and verbena. Add in fresh fruit. Pour in D'oro (or port), wine and club soda. Gently stir and refrigerate at least 1 hour to allow flavors to develop. Serve over ice.

⋇

THREE PERFECT PRESERVES:

Pineapple with Mint & Chile, 106 | Roasted Strawberry & Mint, 37 | Plum with Vanilla & Star Anise, 58

{2.5 LITERS, OR ENOUGH FOR 10 CUPS}

A little old-school, this sweet and spiced version updates the perennial classic. Perfect for après ski and winter holidays.

VISTA D'ORO MULLED WINE

2 750 ml bottles red wine
1 500 ml bottle D'oro
fortified walnut wine
(or port)

1 cup preserves
(suggestions opposite)
Zest and juice of 2 medium
oranges
2 sticks cinnamon

1 vanilla bean, sliced
lengthwise
10 whole star anise
2 Tbsp cardamom pods
1 Tbsp whole pink
peppercorns

1.   Combine all ingredients in a large saucepan. Heat to barely a simmer and keep warm to serve.

VISTA D'ORO MULLED WINE

THREE PERFECT PRESERVES:
Rainier Cherry & Kirsch, 41
Damson Plum & Sweet Vermouth, 51
Mulled Wine Jelly, 102

RESOURCES & GIFTING

RESOURCES

COPPER JAM POTS, JARS AND HARD TO FIND INGREDIENTS

Ball—www.freshpreserving.com

Bernardin—www.bernardin.ca

Gourmet Warehouse—www.gourmetwarehouse.com

Mason jar accessories—www.masonjars.com

Qzina—www.qzina.com

Williams Sonoma Online—www.williams-sonoma.com

Weck Jars—www.weckjars.com

FRIENDS OF THE PRESERVATORY

Benton Brothers Fine Cheese, Granville Island, Vancouver, British Columbia—
www.bentonscheese.com

Driediger Farms, Fraser Valley, British Columbia—www.driedigerfarms.com

Harker's Organics, Similkameen Valley, British Columbia—www.harkersorganics.com

Krause Berry Farms, Fraser Valley, British Columbia—www.krauseberryfarms.com

Les Amis du Fromage, Vancouver, British Columbia—www.buycheese.com

Molto Formaggio, Dallas, Texas—www.moltoformaggio.com

Whole Foods Market, various locations in Canada and the USA—
www.wholefoodsmarket.com

BOOKS WE LOVE

***Culinary Artistry*, by Andrew Dornenburg and Karen Page**—
For failproof flavor pairings

Ball Blue Book Guide to Preserving—For everything that goes in a jar

***On Food and Cooking* by Harold McGee**—To go deep into the science of jam-making

OTHER PRESERVES I HOPE YOU'LL TRY

Christine Ferber—Extraordinary jams from the Alsace. "A batch of jam is always an
act of creation!" says Christine.

June Taylor—Even with her incredible success, June still sells her creations out of her
van at the Ferry Plaza Farmers' Market in San Francisco, because she
loves her community and chooses to continue to support it. Love that!

STOCK-UP PARTY & HOSTESS GIFTS

No other gift is more appreciated than a gift you've made yourself, and if that gift is preserves, even better! The recipient knows you've spent time and thought on the gift and, really, who doesn't love receiving delicious handmade treats?

Culinary hostess gifts can be as simple as a gift box filled with your grandmother's famous oatcakes, or as complex as supplying the recipe and all the ingredients on a beautiful platter for a fabulous hors d'oeuvre, like the Olive & Caramelized Onion Tart.

Many Christmases ago a few of my friends and I started doing "stock-up" parties. The idea was to pool our resources and stock our pantries with decadent treats that we wouldn't normally make the effort to create on our own, or to buy. Cookie exchanges weren't doing it for us anymore. Instead, we put together a menu for the night, each person brought a lovely bottle of wine to share and all went home with decadent treats to be served, gifted or hoarded depending on individual preference. This was also the night Caryn, my awesome head of production, came back into our life and we haven't let her out of the Preservatory since!

Plan your own "stock-up" party; holidays are a great time to get together with your foodie friends and cook up a storm. With schedules being crazy and so little time to socialize, this is a great way to get a little work done and enjoy each other's company at the same time. Be sure to arrange to have everyone bring a nibbly, to go along with the wine, to keep everyone happy and their hands off the "gifts." Choose a date early in the season to get everyone in the holiday spirit and to avoid the crush of the holiday parties.

Once you've chosen a date, and guest list, the fun begins . . . choosing the menu! I like to choose a few things that go well together so you can present a parcel that becomes a delicious snack in a matter of minutes. For a decadent hostess gift the Duck Rillettes (page 159) in porcelain ramekins paired with a jar of Spicy Sweet Charred Onion & Fig preserves (page 86) along with a package of Walnut & Blue Cheese Crackers (page 220) will be a gift they won't soon forget. Another wonderful combination gift of Easy Candied Pecans (page 137) and Raspberry with Chocolate & Brandy preserves (page 43) will put thoughts of yummy late-night sundaes on everyone's mind. Have each guest supply a favorite recipe or two and get a copy of each ahead of time; this will help you plan the market and prep lists.

Once the menu is planned, write up a shopping list and decide how it will be split. You can put one person in charge of all the purchasing or divide it up by category with someone in charge of each area, and this way one person isn't driving around town searching for ingredients all day. The prep list comes next—make it as detailed as possible. I like to estimate time for each step so we know how much time we will have left at the end of the night purely for cleanup; read: gossiping. Also, be sure to make a copy of the recipes for each guest and divide up the tasks equally so everyone gets a chance to get their hands dirty, or the dishes clean.

Take the "stock-up" idea one step further and set up a gift-packaging table. Source beautiful and earth-friendly containers, ribbons and other unique packaging materials and have them laid out and available for everyone to put their imagination to use. Kitchen shops are a great place to start; they are full of containers in different sizes and much more interesting than simple canning jars. There are many stores that specialize in gift packaging, and they always have plenty of new and innovative ideas. Chinese takeout containers are a fun way to package spiced nuts or miniature crackers. You could also check out your local antique dealer for interesting containers or cookie tins—you never know what you'll turn up and it's a perfect way to spend a cold, rainy afternoon. Keep it eco-chic and forgo the plastic and cellophane; parchment paper–wrapped Compound Jam Butters (see page 151) tied with butcher twine are simple and look beautiful. Putting as much thought into the container as you do into what's going in it makes for exceptional gift giving.

The best food gifts always include a recipe, preferably handwritten, and serving suggestions add a nice touch. Have recipe cards and good-quality pens on hand for everyone to do their own to include with each gift.

Truly, the ideas are endless and, like me, you'll find yourself collecting recipes all year long for the much-anticipated annual "stock-up."

Be warned: you may find the party invites doubling once you start bringing your foodie hostess gifts along—as if the holidays weren't already busy enough!

101 Uses for Jam... Please note: There is no toast on this list!

1. Vinaigrette
2. Marinade
3. Stir-fry
4. Ham glaze
5. Fried egg sandwich
6. Charcuterie
7. Ice cream topping
8. Ice cream base
9. Layer cake
10. Cheesecake
11. Pizza (m)
12. Milkshake
13. Gravy
14. Pan sauce
15. Pasta sauce
16. Grilled cheese
17. Crepes
18. Smoothie
19. Trifle
20. Roast chicken
21. Compound butter
22. Burger
23. Meatloaf
24. Cottage cheese
25. Egg salad
26. Granola and yogurt parfait
27. Potato latkes
28. Tea sweetener
29. Yogurt
30. Muffin batter
31. Baked fish
32. Chicken finger dipping sauce
33. Spring roll dipping sauce
34. Oatmeal

35. Cream of wheat
36. Pastry glaze
37. Buttercream icing
38. Jelly roll (obviously)
39. Rugelach
40. Rice pudding
41. Risotto balls
42. Quesadillas
43. Mustard dipping sauce
44. Samosa dip
45. BBQ ribs
46. Chocolate truffle filling
47. Donuts
48. Sandwich cookies
49. Thumbprint cookies
50. Kir Royale base
51. Pound cake
52. Cheese board
53. Cupcakes
54. Meatball sauce
55. Cheese scone
56. Braised cabbage
57. Poultry glaze
58. Grilled pork tenderloin
59. Bread pudding
60. Sandwich
61. Windowpane cookies
62. Panini
63. Pancakes
64. Warm with Brie
65. French toast
66. Short ribs
67. Scrambled eggs and cheese
68. Grilled scallops

69. Pork roast
70. Canapés
71. Sangria
72. Mulled wine
73. Crab cakes
74. Taco
75. Corn tamale
76. Pavlova
77. Eton Mess
78. Mojito
79. Guacamole
80. Fruit salad dressing
81. Tart base
82. Crostini and blue cheese
83. Cheesy grits
84. Bruschetta
85. Sweet and sour sauce
86. BLT & J
87. Veggie burger
88. Fish taco
89. Tuna melt
90. Chicken wings
91. Pulled pork
92. Brussels sprouts
93. Glazed carrots
94. Bagel and cream cheese
95. Cornbread
96. Butternut squash
97. Roast veggies
98. Tuna tataki
99. Chip dip
100. Satay

On your lover (thanks for the suggestion, Chef Van Geest)

ACKNOWLEDGMENTS

Patrick, for eating breakfast for dinner more nights than I'm sure he'd like to remember, for taking care of the menagerie while I sat staring at the screen trying to make the words come out, and for keeping me calm when they weren't!

Morgan, for helping with all the behind-the-scenes chaos and whose farm photos are interspersed throughout the book—you have an amazing talent . . . so proud of you!

Hunter, for being the guinea pig recipe tester and the help in making the recipes even better—your palate is pretty incredible for the amount of craft beer you're consuming at university!

Mum, for your encouragement, support and love of food, which I seem to have inherited directly from you! That and the gift of a KitchenAid mixer along with *Baking with Julia*, which got me started down this crazy road of cooking so long ago now.

Dad, for letting me mess up your kitchen while I tested recipes and being brutally honest about those tests—having *Gunsmoke* on in the background was the icing on the cake!

The Preservatory Squad—Caryn and the Crew, Annette and Nikki—for all their input and bravery during testing—good and bad! I honestly couldn't do what I do without all your help and hard work, as we find out any time one of you goes on holiday and I have to get in there!

Wendy, for lending me so many props and more importantly an ear from the beginning. Turns out her advice to write the book before worrying about the title was very sound.

Becky, for her outstanding food styling on the Brunch chapter—best of the b(r)unch!

Janis and her magic camera, for capturing the feel I was trying to convey and her patience while she waited for me to decide what napkin was going where.

The Appetite by Random House dream team! Jenny, for taking on the, I'm sure, very scary task of working with a newbie, all while making me feel like a veteran. I honestly couldn't imagine getting this book to print without your amazing editing skills and your extreme patience throughout the very long process. Terri, for the beautiful design. It's so beyond the vision I've had—you captured the essence of our farm perfectly!

Caren, the ultimate butt-kicker, for making me hit send on the proposal that I had been hanging on to for over five years and then sending it off to Robert without telling me!

Last but never least, Robert, for taking a chance on me, and for your tireless support and encouragement throughout—so looking forward to our jam-making date!

INDEX

METRIC CONVERSION TABLE

WEIGHT	
½ oz	15 g
1 oz	30 g
2 oz	60 g
3 oz	90 g
4 oz/ ¼ lb	115 g
5 oz	140 g
6 oz	170 g
7 oz	200 g
8 oz/ ½ lb	225 g
12 oz/ ¾ lb	350 g
16 oz/ 1 lb	450 g
2 lb	900 g
2¼ lb	1 kg
3 lb	1.4 kg
4 lb	1.8 kg
5 lb	2.25 kg
6 lb	2.7 kg

VOLUME	
¼ tsp	1 mL
½ tsp	2 mL
1 tsp	5 mL
1 Tbsp	15 mL
1½ Tbsp	22 mL
2 Tbsp	30 mL
3 Tbsp	45 mL
5 Tbsp	75 mL
7 Tbsp	105 mL
¼ cup	60 mL
⅓ cup	75 mL
½ cup	125 mL
⅔ cup	150 mL
¾ cup	175 mL
1 cup	250 mL
1¼ cups	310 mL
1⅓ cups	330 mL
1½ cups	375 mL
2 cups	500 mL
3 cups	750 mL
4 cups	1 L

LENGTH	
⅛ inch	3 mm
¼ inch	6 mm
½ inch	1.2 cm
¾ inch	2 cm
1 inch	2.5 cm
1¼ inches	3 cm
1½ inches	4 cm
2 inches	5 cm
3 inches	8 cm
4 inches	10 cm
5 inches	13 cm
6 inches	15 cm
7 inches	18 cm
8 inches	20 cm
9 inches	23 cm
10 inches	25 cm
11 inches	27 cm
12 inches	30 cm

TEMPERATURE	
200°F	93°C
218°F	103°C
220°F	104°C
225°F	107°C
230°F	110°C
250°F	120°C
275°F	135°C
300°F	150°C
325°F	160°C
350°F	175°C
360°F	180°C
375°F	190°C
400°F	200°C

FLUID VOLUME	
¼ oz	7 mL
½ oz	15 mL
¾ oz	22 mL
1 oz	30 mL
1½ oz	45 mL
2 oz	60 mL
4 oz	120 mL